1

HEALTH CARE ISSUES, COSTS AND ACCESS



# THE AFFORDABLE CARE ACT

## ANALYSES OF EMERGENT ISSUES AND TOPICS

# HEALTH CARE ISSUES, COSTS AND ACCESS

Additional books in this series can be found on Nova's website under the Series tab.

Additional e-books in this series can be found on Nova's website under the e-book tab.

HEALTH CARE ISSUES, COSTS AND ACCESS

# THE AFFORDABLE CARE ACT

## ANALYSES OF EMERGENT ISSUES AND TOPICS


EILEEN H. BLUME
EDITOR



nova publishers
*New York*

For permission to use material from this book please contact us:
Telephone 631-231-7269; Fax 631-231-8175
Web Site: http://www.novapublishers.com



**Library of Congress Cataloging-in-Publication Data**

ISBN: 978-1-63117-871-9

*Published by Nova Science Publishers, Inc. † New York*

# CONTENTS

# PREFACE

The degree to which foreign nationals (noncitizens/aliens) should have access to certain benefits as a result of their presence in the United States, as well as the responsibilities of such persons given their legal status (e.g., immigrants, nonimmigrants, unauthorized aliens), often figures into policy discussions in Congress. These issues become particularly salient when Congress considers legislation to establish new immigration statuses or to create or modify benefit or entitlement programs. This book discusses the Affordable Care Act (ACA), and the emergent issues and topics that arise. It discusses the treatment of noncitizens under the act, as well as individual mandates under the ACA; the delays, extensions, and other actions taken by administration in implementing the ACA; and implications for the ACA.

Chapter 1 - The degree to which foreign nationals (noncitizens/aliens) should be accorded access to certain benefits as a result of their presence in the United States, as well as the responsibilities of such persons given their legal status (e.g., immigrants, nonimmigrants, unauthorized aliens), often figures into policy discussions in Congress. These issues become particularly salient when Congress considers legislation to establish new immigration statuses or to create or modify benefit or entitlement programs.

The 111th Congress enacted the Patient Protection and Affordable Care Act (P.L. 111-148), which has been amended by the Health Care and Education Reconciliation Act of 2010 (P.L. 111-152) and several other bills. (ACA refers to P.L. 111-148 as amended by P.L. 111-152 and the other legislation.) The ACA created new responsibilities (e.g., the requirement that most people in the United States obtain health insurance) and new benefits (e.g., tax credits to help certain people purchase health insurance), and it addressed the eligibility and responsibility of foreign nationals for these provisions. The 113th Congress is considering legislation that would amend or repeal the ACA. In addition, the 113th Congress is considering legislation that would reform the U.S. immigration system, including proposals to create new immigration statuses. One issue that has arisen during some debates to amend provisions in the ACA and during discussions of immigration reform is the eligibility of foreign nationals for some of the ACA's key provisions.

At the center of noncitizen eligibility for provisions under the ACA is the term "lawfully present." Aliens who are "lawfully present in the United States" are generally subject to the health insurance mandate and are eligible, if otherwise qualified, to participate in the exchanges (the health insurance marketplace) and for the premium tax credit and cost-sharing subsidies available to certain individuals who purchase insurance through an exchange. For purposes of the ACA, "lawfully present" has been defined in regulation and includes lawful permanent residents (LPRs), asylees, refugees, foreign nationals admitted under any nonimmigrant visa who are in status, and certain other classifications under the Immigration and Nationality Act (INA).

To purchase insurance through an exchange, a noncitizen must be expected to be lawfully present for the entire period of coverage. Although the minimum period of coverage was established by regulation as 12 months, the exchanges will decide on an enrollment period based on the length of time the alien is authorized to be in the country. The ACA bars foreign nationals who are not lawfully present from purchasing insurance through a health insurance exchange.

In addition, certain individuals who purchase insurance through an exchange may be eligible for the premium tax credit and cost-sharing subsidies to help defray the cost of the insurance. To be eligible, an applicant must meet income requirements based on family size and the federal poverty level, and must also file a tax return in order to claim the credit. Noncitizens who are not lawfully present are ineligible for the premium credit and cost-sharing subsidies because they are barred from purchasing insurance through an exchange.

To enforce the noncitizen eligibility requirements under the ACA, the act required the Secretary of Health and Human Services to establish a program to determine whether an individual who is to be covered in the individual market by a qualified health plan offered through an exchange or who is claiming a premium tax credit or cost-sharing subsidy is a citizen or national of the United States or an alien lawfully present in the United States. This system first checks the Social Security Administration (SSA) records. If SSA can confirm that the person is a citizen, then the check stops at that point. If the person is a "noncitizen" in SSA records, the system checks against Department of Homeland Security (DHS) records to confirm lawful presence. The Departments of Health and Human Services and Homeland Security have stated that no information collected as part of enrollment in an exchange plan will be used for any civil immigration enforcement actions.

Chapter 2 - Beginning in 2014, ACA requires most individuals to maintain health insurance coverage or otherwise pay a penalty. Specifically, most individuals will be required to maintain minimum essential coverage, which is a term defined in ACA and its implementing regulations and includes most private and public coverage (e.g., employer-sponsored coverage, individual coverage, Medicare, and Medicaid, among others). Some individuals will be exempt from the mandate and the penalty, while others may receive financial assistance to help them pay for the cost of health insurance coverage and the costs associated with using health care services.

Individuals who do not maintain minimum essential coverage and are not exempt from the mandate will have to pay a penalty for each month of noncompliance with the mandate. The penalty is the greater of a flat dollar amount or a percentage of applicable income. In 2014, the annual penalty is the greater of $95 or 1% of applicable income; the penalty increases in 2015 and 2016 and is adjusted for inflation thereafter. The penalty will be collected through federal income tax returns. The Internal Revenue Service (IRS) can attempt to collect any owed penalties by reducing the amount of an individual's tax refund; however, individuals who fail to pay the penalty will not be subject to any criminal prosecution or penalty for such failure. The Secretary of the Treasury cannot file notice of lien or file a levy on any property for a taxpayer who does not pay the penalty.

Certain individuals will be exempt from the individual mandate and the penalty. For example, individuals with qualifying religious exemptions and those whose household income is below the filing threshold for federal income taxes will not be subject to the penalty. ACA allows the Secretary of Health and Human Services (HHS) to grant hardship exemptions from the penalty to anyone determined to have suffered a hardship with respect to the capability to obtain coverage. The Secretary of HHS has identified a number of different circumstances that would allow individuals to receive a hardship exemption, including an individual not being eligible for Medicaid based on a state's decision not to carry out the ACA expansion and financial or domestic circumstances that prevent an individual from obtaining coverage (e.g., eviction or recent experience of domestic violence).

ACA includes several reporting requirements designed, in part, to assist individuals in providing evidence of having met the mandate. Every person (including employers, insurers, and government programs) that provides minimum essential coverage to any individual must provide a return to the IRS that includes information about the individual's health insurance coverage.

On March 5, 2014, the House of Representatives passed H.R. 4118, Suspending the Individual Mandate Penalty Law Equals (SIMPLE) Fairness Act. H.R. 4118 provides that individuals do not have to pay an individual mandate penalty for any month prior to January 1, 2015, effectively delaying implementation of the individual mandate penalty and maintaining the initial penalty levels until 2015.

Chapter 3 - This chapter is an edited, reformatted and augmented version of a Congressional Research Service publication R43474, prepared for Members and Committees of Congress, dated April 14, 2014.

Chapter 4 - The Supreme Court's grant of review in *Conestoga Wood Specialties Corp. v. Secretary of U.S. Department of Health and Human Services* and *Hobby Lobby Stores v. Sebelius*, along with recent federal court decisions, has highlighted the ongoing controversy over the scope of the Affordable Care Act's (ACA's) contraceptive coverage requirement, which requires an employer to provide certain contraceptive coverage to its employees under its group health plan. Some employers have objected to the requirement, citing objections to the facilitation of the use of contraceptives in conflict with the religious tenets by which their businesses operate. An analogous issue has arisen in state courts in the context of same-sex weddings. Several private businesses that qualify as public accommodations have objected to state requirements that they provide services without discriminating based on sexual orientation despite the owners' religious objections to same-sex marriage. These issues have raised a novel legal question for the courts: What rights do secular businesses that operate for profit have to pursue legal claims to protect their religious exercise?

Although a number of statutory exemptions exist to protect individuals and organizations' religious beliefs and objections (e.g., employment discrimination under Title VII, disability discrimination under the Americans with Disabilities Act, etc.), courts have applied those exemptions only to individuals and nonprofit, religious organizations. A number of legal challenges to the contraceptive coverage requirement have examined a range of questions related to the rights of these businesses. As a threshold question, courts have had to analyze whether the business itself is eligible for protection under the Religious Freedom Restoration Act (RFRA) and Free Exercise jurisprudence. The businesses have asserted that they qualify as "persons" under RFRA and, in the alternative, that they are entitled to pursue their claims on behalf of their owners under what is known as the "pass-through" theory of corporate rights. Courts have also considered whether the business owners may pursue independent legal claims asserting their objections, or if their individual rights are forfeited at the time of the company's incorporation.

If a court determines that the business or its owners are eligible for free exercise protection, it may then consider the merits of the case, including whether the mandate constitutes a substantial burden on religious exercise; whether the government has a compelling interest to do so; and whether the government used the least restrictive means to achieve that interest. Five federal circuit courts have considered these questions in the context of the contraceptive coverage requirement, and have reached different conclusions on the range of questions raised.

This report examines the constitutional and statutory protections related to free exercise of religion, including current Supreme Court interpretations, as well as judicial and legislative avoidance of defining the parameters of religious belief. It also discusses significant examples of existing religious exemptions in current law, including employment nondiscrimination, health care, and public accommodations law. Finally, it analyzes recent federal judicial decisions that have considered the religious freedom rights of commercial entities whose owners have religious objections to the contraceptive coverage requirement.

jurisprudence. The businesses have asserted that they qualify as "persons" under RFRA and, in the alternative, that they are entitled to pursue their claims on behalf of their owners under what is known as the "pass-through" theory of corporate rights. Courts have also considered whether the business owners may pursue independent legal claims asserting their objections, or if their individual rights are forfeited at the time of the company's incorporation.

If a court determines that the business or its owners are eligible for free exercise protection, it may then consider the merits of the case, including whether the mandate constitutes a substantial burden on religious exercise; whether the government has a compelling interest to do so; and whether the government used the least restrictive means to achieve that interest. Five federal circuit courts have considered these questions in the context of the contraceptive coverage requirement, and have reached different conclusions on the range of questions raised.

This report examines the constitutional and statutory protections related to free exercise of religion, including current Supreme Court interpretations, as well as judicial and legislative avoidance of defining the parameters of religious belief. It also discusses significant examples of existing religious exemptions in current law, including employment nondiscrimination, health care, and public accommodations law. Finally, it analyzes recent federal judicial decisions that have considered the religious freedom rights of commercial entities whose owners have religious objections to the contraceptive coverage requirement.

In: The Affordable Care Act
Editor: Eileen H. Blume

ISBN: 978-1-63117-871-9


*Chapter 1*

# TREATMENT OF NONCITIZENS UNDER THE AFFORDABLE CARE ACT*

***Alison Siskin and Erika K. Lunder***

## SUMMARY

The degree to which foreign nationals (noncitizens/aliens) should be accorded access to certain benefits as a result of their presence in the United States, as well as the responsibilities of such persons given their legal status (e.g., immigrants, nonimmigrants, unauthorized aliens), often figures into policy discussions in Congress. These issues become particularly salient when Congress considers legislation to establish new immigration statuses or to create or modify benefit or entitlement programs.

The 111th Congress enacted the Patient Protection and Affordable Care Act (P.L. 111-148), which has been amended by the Health Care and Education Reconciliation Act of 2010 (P.L. 111-152) and several other bills. (ACA refers to P.L. 111-148 as amended by P.L. 111-152 and the other legislation.) The ACA created new responsibilities (e.g., the requirement that most people in the United States obtain health insurance) and new benefits (e.g., tax credits to help certain people purchase health insurance), and it addressed the eligibility and responsibility of foreign nationals for these provisions. The 113th Congress is considering legislation that would amend or repeal the ACA. In addition, the 113th

* This is an edited, reformatted and augmented version of a Congressional Research Service publication, No. R43561, dated May 21, 2014.

Congress is considering legislation that would reform the U.S. immigration system, including proposals to create new immigration statuses. One issue that has arisen during some debates to amend provisions in the ACA and during discussions of immigration reform is the eligibility of foreign nationals for some of the ACA's key provisions.

At the center of noncitizen eligibility for provisions under the ACA is the term "lawfully present." Aliens who are "lawfully present in the United States" are generally subject to the health insurance mandate and are eligible, if otherwise qualified, to participate in the exchanges (the health insurance marketplace) and for the premium tax credit and cost-sharing subsidies available to certain individuals who purchase insurance through an exchange. For purposes of the ACA, "lawfully present" has been defined in regulation and includes lawful permanent residents (LPRs), asylees, refugees, foreign nationals admitted under any nonimmigrant visa who are in status, and certain other classifications under the Immigration and Nationality Act (INA).

To purchase insurance through an exchange, a noncitizen must be expected to be lawfully present for the entire period of coverage. Although the minimum period of coverage was established by regulation as 12 months, the exchanges will decide on an enrollment period based on the length of time the alien is authorized to be in the country. The ACA bars foreign nationals who are not lawfully present from purchasing insurance through a health insurance exchange.

In addition, certain individuals who purchase insurance through an exchange may be eligible for the premium tax credit and cost-sharing subsidies to help defray the cost of the insurance. To be eligible, an applicant must meet income requirements based on family size and the federal poverty level, and must also file a tax return in order to claim the credit. Noncitizens who are not lawfully present are ineligible for the premium credit and cost-sharing subsidies because they are barred from purchasing insurance through an exchange.

To enforce the noncitizen eligibility requirements under the ACA, the act required the Secretary of Health and Human Services to establish a program to determine whether an individual who is to be covered in the individual market by a qualified health plan offered through an exchange or who is claiming a premium tax credit or cost-sharing subsidy is a citizen or national of the United States or an alien lawfully present in the United States. This system first checks the Social Security Administration (SSA) records. If SSA can confirm that the person is a citizen, then the check stops at that point. If the person is a "noncitizen" in SSA records, the system checks against Department of Homeland Security (DHS) records to confirm lawful presence. The Departments of Health and Human Services and Homeland Security have stated that no information collected as part of enrollment in an exchange plan will be used for any civil immigration enforcement actions.

# INTRODUCTION

The degree to which foreign nationals (noncitizens/aliens)[1] should be accorded access to certain benefits as a result of their presence in the United States, as well as the responsibilities of such persons given their legal status (e.g., immigrants, nonimmigrants, unauthorized aliens), often figures into policy discussions in Congress. These issues become particularly salient when Congress considers legislation to establish new immigration statuses or to create or modify benefit and entitlement programs.

The 111th Congress enacted the Patient Protection and Affordable Care Act (P.L. 111-148), which has been amended by the Health Care and Education Reconciliation Act of 2010 (P.L. 111-152) and several other bills. (ACA refers to P.L. 111-148 as amended by P.L. 111-152 and the other legislation.)[2] The ACA created new responsibilities (e.g., the requirement that most people in the United States obtain health insurance) and new benefits (e.g., tax credits to help certain people purchase health insurance), and it addressed the eligibility and responsibility of foreign nationals for these provisions. The 113th Congress is considering legislation that would amend or repeal the ACA.[3] In addition, the 113th Congress is considering legislation that would reform the U.S. immigration system, including proposals to create new immigration statuses.[4] One issue that has arisen during debates to amend provisions in the ACA and during discussions of immigration reform is the eligibility of foreign nationals for some of the ACA's key provisions.

This report opens with a discussion of several different statutory and regulatory definitions of lawfully present. On the surface, alien eligibility for provisions under the ACA appears straightforward. In general, those who are lawfully present are eligible, and those who are not lawfully present are not eligible. However, due to differing definitions of "lawfully present" and the interaction between the treatment of noncitizens under tax law, the Immigration and Nationality Act, and the ACA, the eligibility of individuals with certain immigration statuses for these provisions can become more complicated.

This report then analyzes the eligibility of foreign nationals for key provisions in the ACA that have restrictions based on immigration status: the requirement to maintain health insurance, the ability to purchase insurance through an exchange, and eligibility for the premium tax credit and cost-sharing subsidies.[5] It includes consideration of the implementing regulations and the impact of the Supreme Court's ruling in *National Federation of Independent Business v. Sebelius*.[6] This report concludes with information on the alien-status verification process and a discussion of select legislation that would affect the eligibility of certain noncitizens for the ACA provisions.

## TREATMENT OF NONCITIZENS UNDER THE PATIENT PROTECTION AND AFFORDABLE CARE ACT (ACA)

The following section discusses alien eligibility for the following provisions under the ACA: the health insurance mandate, the exchanges (the Marketplace), and premium tax credits and cost-sharing subsidies. In general, aliens are separated into two groups for eligibility purposes under the ACA: aliens who are "lawfully present in the United States" are eligible for these provisions, while aliens who are not "lawfully present in the United States" are ineligible.

| |
|---|
| For purposes of this report, the term "not-lawfully present aliens" will refer to noncitizens who do not meet the definition of "lawfully present" under regulations for the ACA. |

### Definition of Lawfully Present

One of the complexities of alien eligibility for the ACA stems from the difficulty of defining who is considered lawfully present. The regulations implementing the ACA define lawfully present to include immigrants, asylees/refugees, nonimmigrants, and most other noncitizens who are known to the U.S. government and have been given some type of permission to remain temporarily in the United States. (For the full list, see **Appendix A**). "Lawfully present" was first defined by regulation in this context for the purposes of eligibility for the high risk pools for uninsured people with pre-existing conditions.[7] Since then, all regulations regarding the ACA have referenced that definition for the health insurance mandate, the exchanges, and the premium credit and cost-sharing subsidies.[8] The definition of lawfully present for the ACA is identical to the Center for Medicaid and Medicare Services (CMS) policy definition of "lawfully residing" for Medicaid and CHIP eligibility[9] and is similar to the definition of "lawfully present" for Social Security eligibility.[10]

Nonetheless, “lawfully present” is not a term that is widely used within the Immigration and Nationality Act (INA). The INA divides foreign nationals into two general types of legal statuses for admission to the United States: immigrants and nonimmigrants. Under the INA, other aliens may have permission to be in the United States, but they do not have an immigration status. The term “lawfully present” in the INA is only defined in regards to noncitizen eligibility for Social Security.[11] The INA also defines the term “unlawfully present” specifically for purposes of determining inadmissibility, but that definition is not equivalent to the definition of “lawfully present” for purposes of the ACA.[12]

There are noncitizens who have temporary permission to remain in the Unites States under narrowly defined circumstances such as those with temporary protected status (TPS),[13] withholding of removal,[14] Deferred Enforced Departure,[15] and parole[16]—often referred to as the “quasi-legal population.” This “quasi-legal” population is counted by researchers at the Department of Homeland Security (DHS) and at the Pew Research Center’s Hispanic Trends Project—the two main entities that estimate the unauthorized alien population—as part of the unauthorized (illegal) population. Although these “quasi-legal” migrants comprise a small percentage of the total noncitizen population, most are considered “lawfully present” for the purposes of the ACA.[17] (For a discussion of these estimates, see **Appendix B**, “Estimates of the Noncitizen Population in the United States.”)

## Health Insurance Mandate

The ACA includes the “individual mandate,” which generally requires individuals to have a minimum level of health insurance beginning in 2014 and imposes penalties for noncompliance.[18] In other words, most individuals who do not maintain a minimum level of health insurance coverage for themselves and their dependents will be required to pay a penalty, which is administered and collected through the Internal Revenue Code (IRC). The ACA and its implementing regulations identify some exemptions from the mandate.[19]

For those who do not maintain coverage and do not qualify for an exemption, the penalties will be assessed through the federal tax filing process. If an individual fails to pay the penalty, the Internal Revenue Service (IRS) can collect any penalties owed by reducing the amount of an individual’s tax refund, but is prohibited from using other common methods of collection (e.g., garnishing the individual's wages).[20]

Aliens are expressly exempted from the individual mandate for any month they are not lawfully present in the United States.[21] Additionally, a noncitizen who is a nonresident alien (which is a term used in tax law and is defined below in "Tax Treatment of Noncitizens") is also exempt from the individual mandate.[22] Nonresident aliens include both lawfully and non-lawfully present individuals.

All other aliens who are lawfully present and are not nonresident aliens are covered by the requirement to maintain health insurance, provided they do not qualify for an exemption.[23]

### Tax Treatment of Noncitizens

For purposes of the ACA, understanding the U.S. income tax treatment of noncitizens may be important for several reasons, including that any noncitizen who is a nonresident alien—which is a tax law term—is not subject to the individual mandate.[24] Also, some might be interested in understanding the tax liability of noncitizens in light of the fact that the IRS may face difficulty in enforcing the mandate against any taxpayer (citizen or resident alien) who does not receive a tax refund.

For federal tax purposes, foreign nationals are classified as resident or nonresident aliens.[25] These terms are used in the Internal Revenue Code (IRC) but do not exist in the Immigration and Nationality Act (INA).[26] As a result, the specific immigration statuses under the INA do not align directly with the terms resident and nonresident alien.[27]

In general, an individual is a nonresident alien unless he or she meets the qualifications under either residency test:

- Green card test: the individual is a lawful permanent resident of the United States at any time during the current year, or
- Substantial presence test: the individual is present in the United States for at least 31 days during the current year and at least 183 days during the current year and previous two years (counting all the qualifying days in the current year, one-third of the days in the prior year, and one-sixth of the days in the earliest year).[28]

There are several situations in which an individual may be classified as a nonresident alien even though he or she meets the substantial presence test. For example, an individual will generally be treated as a nonresident alien if he or she has a closer connection to a foreign country than to the United States, maintains a "tax home" in the foreign country, and is in the United States for fewer than 183 days during the year.[29] Another example is that an individual in the United States under an F-, J-, M-, or Q-visa—students, teachers, trainees, and cultural exchange visitors—may be treated as a nonresident alien if he or she has substantially complied with visa requirements.[30] This treatment generally applies to foreign students (most foreign students are on F visas) for their first five years in the United States and to teachers and trainees for the first two years.[31]

Additional examples of individuals who may be treated as nonresident aliens even if they would otherwise meet the substantial presence test include regular commuters from Canada or Mexico, among others.[32] Furthermore, depending on where the individual is from, there may be an income tax treaty between that country and the United States with provisions for determining residency status.[33]

Resident aliens are subject to the same tax treatment as U.S. citizens, which includes being subject to tax on income from both U.S. and foreign sources. They are subject to the same rules as U.S. citizens regarding income tax withholding and making estimated tax payments throughout the year. To the extent such withholding or payments exceed an individual's income tax liability, he or she may receive a tax refund from the IRS, which could be reduced to collect the penalty for failure to comply with the individual mandate.

Nonresident aliens are subject to different treatment.[34] For example, some income earned by nonresident aliens is excluded from gross income and thus U.S. taxation, including foreign-source income, compensation paid by a foreign employer to a nonresident alien with a F, J, or Q-visa, compensation of employees of foreign governments and international organizations, and income exempt under an income tax treaty or other agreement.[35] Since nonresident aliens are not subject to the individual mandate and therefore would not owe the penalty, their withholding and refund rules do not appear to be relevant.

## Exchanges

The ACA allows certain individuals and small businesses to buy health insurance through state exchanges. (The exchanges are also called health insurance marketplaces.) The exchanges are not themselves insurers, but rather are special marketplaces where insurance firms may sell health insurance policies that meet federally established guidelines to eligible individuals and small businesses.[36] Under the ACA, the open enrollment period for exchanges began October 1, 2013. The law allows all lawfully present noncitizens to purchase insurance through an exchange, but specifies that a person is only considered lawfully present if the person is, and is reasonably expected to be for the entire period of enrollment, a U.S. citizen or national or an alien who is lawfully present in the United States.[37]

Although the shortest period of enrollment has been established by regulation as 12 months,[38] the Department of Health and Human Services (HHS) has indicated that an exchange will determine an individual's eligibility for the period of time for which the individual's lawful presence has been verified. HHS also stated that it may issue additional guidance on this topic.[39] As of the date of this report, CRS is not aware of such guidance. In other words, it appears that all lawfully present noncitizens, regardless of the length of admittance to the United States, are able to purchase insurance through an exchange.

Aliens who are not lawfully present are barred from obtaining insurance through an exchange.[40]

### Premium Tax Credit and Cost-Sharing Subsidies

Based on their income, certain individuals may qualify for a tax credit toward their premium costs and a subsidy for their cost-sharing for insurance purchased through an exchange.[41] The tax credit is both (1) refundable, meaning it can exceed a taxpayer's income tax liability, with the taxpayer receiving the difference as a cash payment from the IRS in the form of a tax refund (and therefore it can be claimed by taxpayers with little or no U.S. income tax liability) and (2) advanceable, meaning the taxpayer can claim it when he or she files an income tax return at the end of the year or claim advance payment of it, in which case the credit will go directly to the insurer.[42] The subsidies go toward cost-sharing expenses, such as coinsurance and co-payments, and are paid to the insurance company and not directly to the enrollee.[43]

In order to claim the credit or subsidy, an individual's household income generally must be at least 100% but no more than 400% of the applicable federal poverty level (FPL). Household income is the family's adjusted gross income plus any excluded foreign income/housing costs, tax-exempt interest, and non-taxable Social Security benefits.[44] Additionally, the individual must not have access to affordable coverage from alternate sources, such as Medicaid or employer provided coverage.[45]

All lawfully present aliens who meet specified criteria are eligible for the premium tax credit and cost-sharing subsidies.[46] Further, there is a special rule for them—household income that is less than 100% of FPL will be deemed to be 100% if the individual or a member of his/her family is a lawfully present alien and is not eligible for Medicaid due to alien status (discussed further below in "ACA Changes to Medicaid").[47]

Aliens who are not lawfully present are ineligible for the tax credit and subsidies. This is because the credit and subsidy are only available for months during which a person purchases health insurance through the exchanges and aliens who are not lawfully present are prohibited from buying insurance through an exchange. However, an individual who is not lawfully present may claim the credit or subsidy for an eligible family member.[48] Thus, for example, a not-lawfully present parent may file a tax return claiming the premium credit if he or she has children who meet the credit's qualifications.

In addition, the law provides specific rules for calculating the credits and subsidies for mixed-status families—families where at least one member is an unlawfully present alien and at least one member is lawfully present or a U.S. citizen.[49] For these families, the premiums used to compute the value of the credit and subsidies are reduced by any amount attributable to the non-lawfully present individual(s). Additionally, for determining whether the family meets the income/FPL criteria, family size and household income are reduced to account for the excluded family member(s).[50] For example, if a family of three has one member who is not lawfully present, the household income eligibility will be based on the FPL for a family of two and the family's household income will be adjusted to account for the not-lawfully present member.

## ACA Changes to Medicaid

Prior to the ACA, federal law generally required state Medicaid plans to cover certain low income individuals, such as the aged, blind, disabled, or members of families with dependent children. The ACA, as enacted, required state Medicaid programs to expand coverage to all eligible nonpregnant, non-elderly legal residents with incomes effectively up to 138% of the federal poverty level (FPL), or risk losing their federal Medicaid matching funds. However, in *National Federation of Independent Business v. Sebelius*,[51] the

Supreme Court held that the withdrawal of all Medicaid funds from the states for failure to comply with the expansion of the program violated the Tenth Amendment (but also found that the withholding of just the funds associated with that expansion raised no significant constitutional concerns).

Reportedly, as of March 28, 2014, twenty-six states and the District of Columbia have expanded Medicaid coverage, and another three states are considering expanding coverage.[52] Several states have indicated that they will not expand Medicaid coverage.[53] Thus, in 26 states and the District of Columbia all non-elderly U.S. *citizens* and certain noncitizens with income effectively up to 138% FPL are eligible for Medicaid.[54] This reform not only expanded eligibility to a group that was not historically eligible for Medicaid (low-income childless adults), but it also raised Medicaid's mandatory income eligibility level for certain existing groups (e.g., individuals with disabilities and children age 6 through 18) to 133% of the FPL (effectively 138% of FPL) and is considered by some to be the most significant expansion of Medicaid eligibility in many years.[55]

Nonetheless, neither the ACA nor the *NFIB v. Sebelius* decision amended the current immigration status-based restrictions (i.e., alien eligibility requirements) on receiving Medicaid.

Under the Personal Responsibility and Work Opportunity Reconciliation Act of 1996 (PRWORA),[56] as amended, noncitizens' eligibility for Medicaid largely depends on their *immigration status*, whether they arrived in the United States (or were on a program's rolls) before *August 22, 1996*,[57] and how long they have lived and worked in the United States. Notably, to be eligible for Medicaid, aliens must also meet the program's financial and categorical eligibility requirements.[58] Most legal permanent residents (LPRs) entering the United States after August 22, 1996, are barred from Medicaid for five years, after which time they are eligible at the state's option. However, states may also choose to use state and federal Medicaid funds to cover pregnant women and children who are "lawfully residing" in the United States.[59] In addition, states have the option to use state-only funds to provide medical coverage for LPRs within five years of their arrival in the United States.[60]

Refugees and asylees[61] are eligible for Medicaid for seven years after arrival. After this period, they may be eligible for Medicaid at the state's option.[62] Qualified aliens with a substantial (10- year) U.S. work history or a military connection are eligible for Medicaid without regard to the five-year bar. Similarly, qualified aliens receiving Supplemental Security Income (SSI) on or after August 22, 1996, are eligible for Medicaid.[63] Nonimmigrants, "quasi-legal" migrants,[64] and aliens present without authorization are barred from Medicaid.[65] However, states may choose to cover these individuals using state-only funds.[66]

### Interaction Between Alien Eligibility for Premium Credits/Subsidies and Medicaid Eligibility

Some have raised concerns that the ACA created an inequality between U.S. citizens and some noncitizens with incomes at or below 138% of the federal poverty level (FPL) with respect to eligibility to participate in an exchange and receive premium tax credits or cost-sharing subsidies.[67] The following section explores the possible differences in treatment between Medicaid-eligible U.S. citizens and noncitizens as compared to Medicaid-ineligible noncitizens.

As discussed, beginning January 1, 2014, qualifying individuals may receive refundable tax credits and cost-sharing subsidies toward the purchase of an exchange plan. To be eligible for the premium credits and subsidies, a taxpayer must have a household income that is above 100% of the FPL but does not exceed 400% of the FPL, and must not have access to affordable coverage outside of an exchange.[68] In addition, lawfully present noncitizens who have household incomes that do not exceed 100% of the FPL and who are ineligible for Medicaid due to their alien status will be deemed to have income at 100% of the FPL and therefore will be *eligible* for premium credits and subsidies. Notably, if a person who applies for premium credits in an exchange is determined to be eligible for Medicaid, the exchange will have that person enrolled in Medicaid.[69]

Under the ACA, lawfully present noncitizens (including some LPRs within five years of entry) who are ineligible for Medicaid due to their alien status are eligible to participate in an exchange and receive premium credits and cost-sharing subsidies.[70] Similarly situated U.S. citizens and lawfully present noncitizens who are eligible for Medicaid could technically participate in an exchange, but they would be ineligible for the premium credits and cost-sharing subsidies.[71]

## VERIFICATION OF ALIEN STATUS UNDER THE ACA

To enforce the alien eligibility requirements under the act, Section 1411 of the ACA requires the Secretary of Health and Human Services (HHS) to establish a program to determine whether an individual who is to be covered through an exchange plan or who is claiming a premium tax credit or reduced cost-sharing is a citizen or national of the United States or an alien lawfully present in the United States.[72] This requirement is similar to and compatible with the Department of Homeland Security (DHS) Systematic Alien Verification for Entitlements (SAVE) system established by Section 1137(d) of the Social Security Act.[73]

The verification system created under the ACA uses three pieces of personal data to verify citizenship and immigration status.[74] The Social Security Administration (SSA) verifies the name, social security number, and date of birth of the individual. For those attesting to be U.S. citizens, the attestation is considered substantiated if it is consistent with SSA data. For individuals who do not claim to be U.S. citizens but attest to be lawfully present in the United States, the attestation is considered substantiated if it is consistent with DHS data.[75] The ACA requires such verification of all individuals seeking exchange coverage regardless of whether they would be federally subsidized or would pay premiums entirely on their own.

Some argue that because the proposed verification system does not include a biometric identifier,[76] it could lead to identity theft; however, requiring applicants to provide documents with biometric identifiers could lead to the inappropriate denial of credits and subsidies to eligible persons.[77] The system only verifies that the name, SSN, and date of birth match the SSA's records and that immigration documents match DHS records; as a result, a person (e.g., a U.S. citizen, a not-lawfully present alien) who is using the documents of an eligible person would not necessarily be denied access to an exchange or disallowed the premium credit and cost-sharing subsidies.[78] Nonetheless, while all lawfully present noncitizens have documents with biometric identifiers,[79] U.S. citizens do not necessarily have such documents,[80] and, as a result, requiring such biometric identifiers could make it more difficult for some eligible U.S. citizens to gain access to an exchange and to claim the premium credits and cost-sharing subsidies.[81]

In a recent evaluation of the E-Verify system for employment, a system that is often compared to the new system under the ACA because it electronically verifies both U.S. citizens and noncitizens, researchers estimate that 6.2% of all queries relate to unauthorized aliens, and that in about half (54%) of these queries the unauthorized aliens receive an inaccurate finding of being work-authorized, primarily due to identity theft. Thus, the researchers estimate that about 3.3% of all queries receive a false positive verification. In other words, it is estimated that of the unauthorized aliens that are run through the system, approximately 54% who are using false documents are not identified by the system.[82] In an effort to better detect and deter identity fraud,

DHS (which administers E-Verify) is taking steps that include adding more photographs to the system and developing methods to prevent stolen identities from being used in the system.[83]

## Immigration Enforcement and Verification for Exchange Plans

One concern that has been raised is that noncitizens who are part of mixed-status families, (i.e., families where at least one member of the family is not authorized to be in the United States) may not apply for coverage through an exchange or for the credits and subsidies because they are worried that their application may trigger an immigration enforcement action.[84] DHS has stated that it will not use information obtained for determining eligibility as the basis for "pursuing a civil immigration enforcement action against such individuals or members of their household."[85]

**In addition, under regulation, exchange plan applications "m**ay not request information regarding citizenship, status as a national, or immigration status for an individual who is not seeking coverage for himself or herself on any application or supplemental form."[86]

In addition, some immigrant advocates have expressed concerns that noncitizens may be hesitant to enroll in an exchange plan and apply for premium credits and cost-sharing subsidies because it may trigger the "public charge" ground of inadmissibility and deportability.[87] An FAQ released by the Obama Administration states:

> Applying for Medicaid or CHIP, or getting help with health insurance costs in the Marketplace [through an exchange], does not make someone a "public charge." It will not affect someone's chances of becoming a Lawful Permanent Resident or U.S. citizen. The one exception is for people receiving long-term care in an institution at government expense. These people may face barriers [obtaining LPR status].[88]

# LEGISLATION IN THE 113TH CONGRESS

This section addresses selected legislation in the 113th Congress that would affect the eligibility of certain noncitizens for key provisions of the ACA.

## S. 744, As Passed by the Senate

On June 27, 2013, the Senate passed the Border Security, Economic Opportunity, and Immigration Modernization Act (S. 744).[89] Among numerous other changes to immigration law, S. 744 would provide pathways for unauthorized aliens to legalize by adjusting to one of the proposed new statuses—"registered provisional immigrant" (RPI) status and "blue card" status— and ultimately legal permanent resident (LPR) status after specified border security and interior enforcement criteria are met. In addition, the bill would make nonimmigrant V visas available to all persons with approved petitions pending within a family preference category.[90]

S. 744 would exclude short-term visitors for business or pleasure (B visas) and foreign students (F visas) from being considered lawfully present for the purposes of the Children's Health Insurance Program (CHIP) option for states to cover pregnant women and children. S. 744 would further specify that all other U.S. Department of Health and Human Service (HHS) and Department of Treasury "health-related programs" that use the term "lawfully present" should reflect these restrictions.[91] In other words, S. 744 as passed by the Senate would direct the Secretaries of HHS and Treasury to amend the definition of lawfully present for eligibility under the ACA to exclude short-term visitors and foreign students.

S. 744 would also limit the access of aliens who legalize under the bill and those in V visa status to certain benefits provided by the ACA. Aliens with RPI, blue card, or V statuses would be considered lawfully present for all purposes under S. 744, except that they would not be entitled to the premium tax credit or cost sharing subsidies, and they would be exempt from the individual mandate to have health insurance.[92] Such aliens would be eligible, however, to purchase insurance through an exchange without any credits or subsidies.

### S. 744 and the Employer Mandate

An issue that has been raised in relation to S. 744 is whether the proposed prohibition on receiving credits or subsidies would create an incentive for employers to hire RPIs, blue card holders, and V visa holders instead of U.S. citizens and other foreign nationals since such aliens cannot trigger the employer penalties.[93] Nonetheless, there are other provisions in law, such as the requirement that "similarly situated individuals" must be treated the same under a health plan,[94] and the ACA's prohibition of discrimination in favor of highly compensated individuals,[95] that might possibly lessen or negate any such incentive.

To ensure that employers continue to provide some degree of health insurance coverage, the ACA includes a "shared responsibility" provision. This provision does not explicitly mandate that an employer offer employees health insurance; however, the ACA imposes penalties on "large" employers if at least one of their full-time employees obtains a premium credit through an exchange. An employer who employs on average at least 50 full-time equivalents (FTEs) is defined as a "large" employer.[96]

In terms of the employer mandate, RPIs, V visa holders, and those in blue card status cannot trigger the penalty since they would be ineligible for premium credits. Nonetheless, RPIs and those in blue card or V statuses would be included in the calculation to determine the size of the employer's workforce (i.e., if an RPI is considered an "employee" and not an independent contractor then his hours would be included in the FTE calculation).

If an employer is subject to the penalty, the amount of the penalty depends on whether the employer provides coverage or not.

- If the employer does not offer coverage and one of its full-time employees enters an exchange and receives a premium credit than the employer is liable for an annual penalty of $2,000 times (# of FT workers - 30). In this case a full-time RPI/blue card holder/V visa holder could be included in the penalty calculation because he is a full-time worker (even though he could not "trigger" the penalty).
- If the employer offers coverage but the coverage is inadequate or unaffordable[97] and one of its employees revives a premium credit toward exchange coverage, then the annual penalty is the lesser of:
  - $2,000 times (# of FT workers - 30); or
  - $3,000 times (# of FT workers who receive premium credits).

In these cases, a full-time RPI/blue card holder/V visa holder would be included in the former calculation but not the latter.

## H.R. 4414, As Passed by the House

The Expatriate Health Coverage Clarification Act (H.R. 4414) was passed by the House on April 29, 2014.[98] The bill would specify that expatriate health insurance plans do not have to comply with the ACA. An expatriate plan would be one in which substantially all of the primary enrollees in such a plan or coverage are qualified expatriates. Under the bill, many foreign nationals in the United States, regardless of immigration status, would be considered qualified expatriates.

# APPENDIX A. DEFINITION OF LAWFULLY PRESENT UNDER THE ACA

"Lawfully present" was first defined for the purposes of eligibility for the high risk pools for uninsured people with pre-existing conditions.[99] Since then, all regulations regarding the ACA have referenced that definition.[100]

For the provisions of the ACA, "lawfully present" means

1. A qualified alien as defined in Section 431 of the Personal Responsibility and Work Opportunity Act (PRWORA);[101]

2. An alien in nonimmigrant status[102] who has not violated the terms of the status under which he or she was admitted or to which he or she has changed after admission;

3. An alien who has been paroled into the United States under INA Section 212(d)(5)[103] for less than one year, except for an alien paroled for prosecution, for deferred inspection or pending removal proceedings;

4. An alien who belongs to one of the following classes:

Aliens currently in temporary resident status pursuant to INA §210 or 245A;[104]

Aliens currently under Temporary Protected Status (TPS),[105] and pending applicants for TPS who have been granted employment authorization;

Aliens who have been granted employment authorization under 8 CFR 274a.12(c)(9), (10), (16), (18), (20), (22), or (24);

Family Unity beneficiaries pursuant to Section 301 of P.L. 101-649 as amended; Aliens currently under Deferred Enforced Departure (DED);

Aliens currently in deferred action status except an individual with deferred action under the DHS's deferred action for childhood arrivals process, as described in the Secretary of Homeland Security's June 15, 2012, memorandum, shall not be considered to be lawfully present;

Aliens whose visa petitions have been approved and who have a pending application for adjustment of status;

5. A pending applicant for asylum under INA Section 208(a)[106] or for withholding of removal under INA Section 241(b)(3)[107] or under the Convention Against Torture who has been granted employment authorization, and such an applicant under the age of 14 who has had an application pending for at least 180 days;

6. An alien who has been granted withholding of removal under the Convention Against Torture; or

7. A child who has a pending application for Special Immigrant Juvenile status.[108]

# APPENDIX B. THE ESTIMATED SIZE OF THE NONCITIZEN POPULATION IN THE UNITED STATES

Using the 2012 American Community Survey 1-Year Estimates,[109] the Congressional Research Service (CRS) estimated that as of July 2012 there were approximately 40.8 million foreign-born persons in the United States, approximately 13% of the U.S. population.[110] The foreign-born population was comprised of approximately 18.7 million naturalized U.S. citizens[111] and 22.1 million noncitizens.[112]

CRS does not estimate the unauthorized (illegal) alien population;[113] however, the Pew Research Center's Hispanic Trends Project[114] produces estimates of the number of unauthorized aliens[115] in the United States. Researchers at the Pew Hispanic Trends Project used the same data as CRS but adjusted the survey weights to account for perceived noncitizen undercounts in the survey.[116] They also assigned a specific immigration status (e.g., legal permanent resident, unauthorized alien) to each foreign-born survey respondent and used a methodology to estimate the illegally present population.[117]

The Pew Hispanic Trends Project estimated that in March 2012 there were approximately 41.7 million foreign-born persons in the United States, and of the noncitizen population, approximately 28.3 million were legal permanent residents (LPRs) and naturalized citizens, 1.7 million were temporarily in the United States (i.e., nonimmigrants), and 11.7 million (28%) were estimated to be unauthorized (illegal) aliens.[118]

## "Quasi-Legal" Migrants

Not all unauthorized aliens lack legal documents, leading many observers to characterize these *documented* aliens as "quasi-legal" migrants.[119] According to the researchers at PEW, data on this population are very limited, but this "quasi-legal" group could account for as much as 10% of the unauthorized population.[120] Specifically, there are certain circumstances in which the Department of Homeland Security issues temporary employment authorization documents (EADs) to aliens who are not otherwise considered authorized to reside in the United States. Aliens with EADs, in turn, may legally obtain social security cards.[121] These "quasi-legal" unauthorized aliens fall in several categories:

- The government has given them temporary humanitarian relief from removal, such as Temporary Protected Status (TPS).[122]
- They have sought asylum in the United States and their cases have been pending for at least 180 days.[123]
- They are immediate family or fiancées of legal permanent residents (LPRs) who are awaiting in the United States their legal permanent residency cases to be processed.[124]
- They have overstayed their nonimmigrant visas and have petitions pending to adjust status as employment-based LPRs.[125]

None of the aliens described above have been formally approved to remain in the United States permanently, and many with pending cases may ultimately be denied LPR status. Only about 25% of asylum seekers, for example, ultimately gain asylum.[126] Approximately 80% to 85% of LPR petitions reportedly are approved.[127]

Importantly for the discussion of the ACA, some of the noncitizens included in the estimates of "unauthorized aliens" are considered lawfully present under the ACA regulations (see the discussion entitled "Definition of Lawfully Present").

## End Notes

[1] A noncitizen is anyone who is not a citizen or national of the United States—this term is synonymous with the terms alien and foreign national. The noncitizen may be in the United States temporarily or permanently and be either lawfully present or present without authorization.

[2] The ACA was signed into law on March 23, 2010. On March 30, 2010, the ACA was amended by P.L. 111-152, the Health Care and Education Reconciliation Act of 2010. Since then, Congress has passed more than 10 laws that amend the ACA. None of the legislation enacted after P.L. 111-148 changed the eligibility of noncitizens for the key provisions of the ACA discussed in this report. For a discussion of the legislation to amend the ACA, see CRS Report R43289, *Legislative Actions to Repeal, Defund, or Delay the Affordable Care Act*, by C. Stephen Redhead and Janet Kinzer.

[3] For example, see in the 113th Congress, H.R. 45, H.R. 3350, and H.R. 4414.

[4] See S. 744 in the 113th Congress.

[5] For more information on these provisions, see CRS Report R41331, *Individual Mandate Under ACA*, by Annie L. Mach; CRS Report R43233, *Private Health Plans Under the ACA: In Brief*, by Bernadette Fernandez and Annie L. Mach; CRS Report R42663, *Health Insurance Exchanges Under the Patient Protection and Affordable Care Act (ACA)*, by Bernadette Fernandez and Annie L. Mach; and CRS Report R41137, *Health Insurance Premium Credits in the Patient Protection and Affordable Care Act (ACA)*, by Bernadette Fernandez.

[6] *National Federation of Independent Business v. Sebelius*, 132 S. Ct. 2566 (2012). For more information, see CRS Legal Sidebar WSLG108, *A Line in Shifting Sand?: Failure to Implement "New" Medicaid Requirements Under the ACA Cannot Result in Loss of Existing Funds*, by Kenneth R. Thomas; CRS Report R42367, *Medicaid and Federal Grant Conditions After NFIB v. Sebelius: Constitutional Issues and Analysis*, by Kenneth R. Thomas.

[7] 45 C.F.R. §152.2; 75 Fed. Reg. 45029, July 30, 2010, as amended by 77 Fed. Reg. 52616, Aug. 30, 2012.

[8] 26 C.F.R. §§1.36B-1(g), 1.5000A-3(c)(2)(ii)(B); 45 C.F.R. §155.20. See also 42 C.F.R. §600.5 (using the same definition for the basic health program).

[9] Center for Medicare and Medicaid Services, Re: Medicaid and CHIP Coverage of "Lawfully Residing" Children and Pregnant Women, SHO # 10-006, CHIPRA #1 7, Baltimore, MD, July 1, 2010, http://downloads.cms.gov/cmsgov/archived-downloads/SMDL/downloads /SHO10006.pdf.

[10] 8 C.F.R. §103.12. For a discussion of noncitizen eligibility for Social Security, see CRS Report RL32004, *Social Security Benefits for Noncitizens*, by Dawn Nuschler and Alison Siskin.

[11] P.L. 104-208 (The Illegal Immigration Reform and Immigrant Responsibility Act of 1996) amended the INA to state that only lawfully present noncitizens are eligible to receive Social Security benefits in the United States. Lawfully present for Social Security eligibility is defined in regulation (8 C.F.R. §103.12). The definition is similar to the definition of lawfully present under the ACA. In addition, P.L. 104-193, (The Personal Responsibility and Welfare Reform Act of 1996), also contains a provision that requires states to pass a law if they want to provide state or local public benefits to aliens who are not lawfully present (§411(d)). Nonetheless, there is not a definition associated with "not lawfully present" for this purpose. For information on noncitizen eligibility for Social Security, see CRS Report RL32004, *Social Security Benefits for Noncitizens*, by Dawn Nuschler and Alison Siskin.

[12] Unlawfully present is defined in the INA in a very specific manner in §212 (a)(9)(B)(ii) for purposes of that section as: "an alien is deemed to be unlawfully present in the United States if the alien is present in the United States after the expiration of the period of stay authorized by the Attorney General or is present in the United States without being admitted or paroled." 8 U.S.C. §1182(a)(9)(B0(ii).

[13] Temporary Protected Status (TPS) is blanket relief that may be granted under the following conditions: there is ongoing armed conflict posing serious threat to personal safety; a foreign state requests TPS because it temporarily cannot handle the return of nationals due to environmental disaster; or there are extraordinary and temporary conditions in a foreign state that prevent aliens from returning, provided that granting TPS is consistent with U.S. national interests. INA §244(h); 8 U.S.C. §1254a. For more on TPS, see CRS Report RS20844, *Temporary Protected Status: Current Immigration Policy and Issues*, by Ruth Ellen Wasem and Karma Ester.

[14] Withholding of removal is a temporary form of relief from removal to a country where the U.S. government has determined that the alien's life would be threatened because of the alien's race, religion, nationality, membership in a particular social group, or political opinion. INA §214(b)(3), 8 U.S.C. §1231(b)(3). For more on withholding of removal, see CRS Report RL32480, *Immigration Consequences of Criminal Activity*, by Michael John Garcia.

[15] Deferred Enforced Departure (DED) is not and does not confer an immigration status. The granting of DED is not based upon any specific statutory authority, but instead typically premised upon the Executive's independent constitutional authority to provide temporary relief from removal based on foreign policy, humanitarian, and immigration concerns.

[16] "Parole" is a term in the INA which means that the alien has been granted temporary permission to enter and be present in the United States. Parole does not constitute formal admission to the United States and parolees are required to leave when the parole expires, or if eligible, to be admitted in a lawful status. See, for example, 8 C.F.R. §212.5.

[17] See Appendix A, "Definition of Lawfully Present For Purposes of the ACA."

[18] ACA §1501(b) (codified at 26 U.S.C. §5000A). For more information on the health insurance mandate, see CRS Report R41331, *Individual Mandate Under ACA*, by Annie L. Mach.

[19] For more information, see CRS Report R41331, *Individual Mandate Under ACA*, by Annie L. Mach.

[20] ACA §1501(b) (codified at 26 U.S.C. §5000A(g)); 26 C.F.R. §1.5000A-5; Dep't of Treasury, IRS, "Shared Responsibility Payment for Not Maintaining Minimal Essential Coverage," 78 Fed. Reg. 53655 (Aug. 30, 2013) (noting that the accuracy-related penalty for underpayment of tax does not apply to the individual mandate penalty).

[21] ACA §1501(b) (codified at 26 U.S.C. §5000A(d)(3)).

[22] 26 C.F.R. §1.5000A-3(c)(2)(ii)(A).

[23] ACA §1501(b) (codified at 26 U.S.C. §5000A(d)). The requirement only applies to the months that the individual is lawfully present for the entire month. ACA §1501(b) (codified at 26 U.S.C. §5000A(a)).

[24] 26 C.F.R. §1.5000A-3(c)(2)(ii)(A).

[25] It is possible for an individual to be a resident alien and a nonresident alien during the same year. For an explanation of the rules on determining residency starting and ending dates and dual-status filing, see *IRS Publication 519: U.S. Tax Guide for Aliens*, which is available at http://www.irs.gov.

[26] 8 U.S.C. §§1101 *et seq.*

[27] For example, based on time in the United States and treaty obligations, some foreign agricultural workers (H-2A visa holders) would be considered resident aliens while others would be considered nonresident aliens for tax purposes.

[28] 26 U.S.C. §§7701(b)(1)(A) and (b)(3). A nonresident alien may elect, under certain circumstances, to be treated as a resident alien if the substantial presence test is met in the year following the election. 26 U.S.C. §7701(b)(4). A dual-status or nonresident alien

married to a U.S. citizen or resident may qualify to be treated as a resident alien for the entire year. 26 U.S.C. §§6013(g) and (h).

[29] 26 U.S.C. §7701(b)(3)(B).

[30] 26 U.S.C. §7701(b)(5).

[31] 26 U.S.C. §7701(b)(5)(E).

[32] 26 U.S.C. §§7701(b)(3)(D), (b)(5), and (b)(7).

[33] See 26 C.F.R. §301.7701(b)-7.

[34] 26 U.S.C. §872(a).

[35] See, for example, 26 U.S.C. §§892 and 893; Vienna Convention on Consular Relations (April 22, 1963); International Bank For Reconstruction and Development, Articles of Agreement (as amended, effective June 27, 2012).

[36] CRS Report R43243, *Health Insurance Exchanges: Health Insurance "Navigators" and In-Person Assistance*, by Suzanne M. Kirchhoff.

[37] ACA §1312(f)(3) (codified at 42 U.S.C. §18032(f)(3)).

[38] Dep't of Health and Human Services, "Final Rule on Establishment of Exchanges and Qualified Health Plans, and Exchange Standards for Employers, Effective May 29, 2012," 77 Fed. Reg. 18310, March 27, 2012.

[39] In the comment section for the final regulations regarding eligibility for exchanges, HHS states "The final rule maintains the 'reasonably expected' standard in accordance with section 1312(f)(3) of the Affordable Care Act. We do not interpret this provision to mean that an applicant must be lawfully present for an entire coverage year; rather, we anticipate that the verification process will address whether an applicant's lawful presence is time-limited, and if so, the Exchange will determine his or her eligibility for the period of time for which his or her lawful presence has been verified. We anticipate providing future guidance on this topic, with a focus on minimizing administrative complexity and burden." *Ibid,* p. 18350.

[40] ACA §1312(f)(3) (codified at 42 U.S.C. §18032(f)(3)).

[41] ACA §1401(a) (codified at 26 U.S.C. §36B); ACA §1402 (codified at 42 U.S.C. §18071). The credit and subsidies became available in 2014. For more information, see CRS Report R41137, *Health Insurance Premium Credits in the Patient Protection and Affordable Care Act (ACA)*, by Bernadette Fernandez.

[42] For more information, see CRS Report R41137, *Health Insurance Premium Credits in the Patient Protection and Affordable Care Act (ACA)*, by Bernadette Fernandez.

[43] To be eligible, individuals must be eligible for the premium tax credits and enrolled in a silver plan through an exchange. For more information, see CRS Report R43048, *Overview of Private Health Insurance Provisions in the Patient Protection and Affordable Care Act (ACA)*, by Annie L. Mach. See also ACA §1412(a)(3), (b) (codified at 42 U.S.C. 18082(a)(3), (b)).

[44] ACA §§1401(a) and 1412(f)(1) (codified at 26 U.S.C. §36B(d)(2) and 42 U.S.C. 18071(f)(1)).

[45] ACA §1401(a) (codified at 26 U.S.C. §32B(c)(2)(B).

[46] ACA §1401(a) and §1402(f) (codified at 26 U.S.C.. §36B(a) and 42 U.S.C. §18032(f)).

[47] ACA §§1401(a) and 1402(b) (codified at 26 U.S.C. §36B(c)(1)(B) and 42 U.S.C. 18071(b)); 26 C.F.R. §1.36B-2(b)(5).

[48] 26 C.F.R. §§1.36B-2(b)(4).

[49] ACA §§1401(a) and 1402(e)(1)(B) (codified at 26 U.S.C. §36B(e) and 42 U.S.C. §18071(e)); 26 C.F.R. §1.36B-3.

[50] Specifically, family size is reduced by any non-lawfully present individuals and household income is computed by multiplying household income by the ratio of FPL for the adjusted family size to the FPL for the actual family size. The statute and regulations also provide

that the IRS may provide for a "comparable method" for determining the credit for mixed-status families, although the agency has not yet done so. ACA §§1401(a) and 1402(e)(1)(B)(ii) (codified at 26 U.S.C. §36B(e)(1)(B)(ii) and 42 U.S.C. §18071(e)(1)(B)(ii)); 26 C.F.R. §1.36B-3.

[51] *National Federation of Independent Business v. Sebelius*, 132 S. Ct. 2566 (2012). For more information, see CRS Report R42367, *Medicaid and Federal Grant Conditions After NFIB v. Sebelius: Constitutional Issues and Analysis*, by Kenneth R. Thomas.

[52] "Where the States Stand on Medicaid Expansion," *The Daily Briefing*, March 28, 2014, http://www.advisory.com/ Daily-Briefing/Resources/Primers/MedicaidMap. For more information on Medicaid, see CRS Report R43357, *Medicaid: An Overview*, coordinated by Alison Mitchell.

[53] See U.S. Centers for Medicare and Medicaid Services, "Is My State Expanding Medicaid Coverage?" https://www.healthcare.gov/what-if-my-state

[54] The income limit set in law is 133% of FPL; however, it is effectively 138% of the FPL because §1004(e) of P.L. 111-152 requires income equivalent to 5% of the FPL to be disregarded from household income if individuals are at the highest income limits for coverage. 42 C.F.R. §435.603(d)(4).

[55] CRS Report R41210, *Medicaid and the State Children's Health Insurance Program (CHIP) Provisions in ACA: Summary and Timeline*, by Evelyne P. Baumrucker et al.; *Medicaid in a Historic Time of Transformation: Results from a 50-State Medicaid Budget Survey for State Fiscal Years 2013 and 2014,* The Kaiser Commission on Medicaid and the Uninsured, Washington, DC, Oct. 2013, p. 1.

[56] P.L. 104-193, also called the Welfare Reform Act.

[57] The enactment date of PRWORA.

[58] Medicaid is a means-tested entitlement program operated by states within broad federal guidelines. To qualify, an individual must meet both categorical and financial eligibility requirements. Current categorical eligibility requirements relate to the age or other characteristics of an individual. People aged 65 and over, certain persons with disabilities, children and their parents, and pregnant women are among the categories of individuals who may currently qualify. For more on Medicaid eligibility, see CRS Report R43357, *Medicaid: An Overview*, coordinated by Alison Mitchell.

[59] This term has been defined broadly by the Centers for Medicare and Medicaid Services (CMS) and includes qualified aliens as defined in 8 U.S.C. §1641 (i.e., those eligible for federal public benefits, such as LPRs, asylees, and refugees) and aliens in valid nonimmigrant statuses, provided they are residents of the state in which they are applying in order to qualify for Medicaid. For a full list of the immigration categories included in the definition of "lawfully residing in the United States," see Centers for Medicare and Medicaid Services: Center for Medicaid, CHIP and Survey & Certification, *Re: Medicaid and CHIP Coverage of "Lawfully Residing" Children and Pregnant Women*, Department of Health and Human Services, Letter to State Health Officials (SHO # 10-006, CHIPRA # 17), July 1, 2010.

[60] For a detailed discussion of noncitizen eligibility for Medicaid, see pp. 5-7 in CRS Report R40772, *Noncitizen Health Insurance Coverage and Use of Select Safety-Net Providers*, by Alison Siskin.

[61] Refugee and asylee statuses require a finding of persecution or a well-founded fear of persecution in situations of "special humanitarian concern" to the United States. Refugees are admitted from abroad.

[62] 8 U.S.C. §1612(b)(1), (2)(A)(i).

[63] 8 U.S.C. §1612(b)(2)(F).

[64] For a discussion of these noncitizens, see the section entitled "“Quasi-legal” Migrants."

[65] Those with T-visas status (i.e., trafficking victims) are nonimmigrants but are Medicaid eligible.

[66] 8 U.S.C. §1621(d).

[67] For example see John Goodman, "How Do Illegal Immigrants Fare Under ObamaCare?" *National Center for Policy Analysis, John Goodman's Health Policy Blog*, August 10, 2010, http://healthblog.ncpa.org/how-do-illegalimmigrants-fare-under-obamacare/; and Senator Tom Coburn and Senator John Barrasso, *Bad Medicine: A Check-up on the New Federal Health Law*, Washington, DC, July 2010, p. 27, http://coburn.senate.gov/public/index.cfm?a = Files.Serve&File_id=722faf8b-a5be-40fd-a52b-9a98826c1592.

[68] ACA §1401(a) (codified at 26 U.S.C. §32B(c)(2)(B)).

[69] ACA §1311(d)(4)(F) and §1413(a) (codified at 42 U.S.C. §18031(d)(4)(F) and 42 U.S.C. §18083(a)).

[70] ACA §§1401(a) and 1402(b) (codified at 26 U.S.C. §36B(c)(1)(B) and 42 U.S.C. 18071(b)); 26 C.F.R. §1.36B-2(b)(5).

[71] Technically, someone who is Medicaid eligible would be able to decline Medicaid coverage and participate in an exchange. However, they would not be eligible for premium credits or cost-sharing subsidies. Thus, it seems unlikely that a Medicaid-eligible person would choose to or would be able to decline Medicaid coverage and pay for insurance through an exchange.

[72] Codified at 42 U.S.C. §18081.

[73] Codified at 42 U.S.C. §1320b–7. The SAVE system provides federal, state, and local government agencies access to data on immigration status that are necessary to determine noncitizen eligibility for public benefits. DHS does not determine benefit eligibility; rather, SAVE enables the specific program administrators to ensure that only those noncitizens and naturalized citizens who meet their program's eligibility rules actually receive public benefits. The SAVE system does not require a Social Security number (SSN). The key to SAVE is the immigration document number (e.g., number from the individual's permanent resident card, employment authorization document, or I-94 document) and the person's name, date of birth, and nationality. The SAVE system is also the basis for the E-Verify electronic employment eligibility verification system. For more on the SAVE System, see CRS Report R40889, *Noncitizen Eligibility and Verification Issues in the Health Care Reform Legislation*, by Ruth Ellen Wasem. See also, U.S. Citizenship and Immigration Services, "SAVE Governing Laws," Oct. 10, 2012, http://www.uscis.gov/save/aboutsave-program/save-governing-laws

[74] The system is also required to verify income for those individuals claiming the tax credit or cost-sharing subsidies. For individuals who have been issued an SSN, it must be provided to the exchange and is then used by the IRS to verify income in order to determine eligibility and the amount of the credit or subsidy. See, for example, 45 C.F.R. §155.320(c). Noncitizens who are ineligible for SSNs file their taxes using an Individual Taxpayer ID Number (ITIN) and they will generally have to provide other proof of income to enroll in an exchange plan. In addition, if a member of a mixed status family is eligible for a tax credit, the household must file a tax return (either using an SSN or ITIN depending on the circumstances) for the year the person has coverage. 26 U.S.C. §§6011 6012; 26 C.F.R. §1.6011-8; 45 C.F.R. §155.305(f)(4). Also see discussion at 77 Fed. Reg. 18355 (Mar. 27, 2012). For more on ITINs, see CRS Report R42628, *Ability of Unauthorized Aliens to Claim Refundable Tax Credits*, by Erika K. Lunder et al. See also 45 C.F.R. §155.310(a)(3) (providing that individuals who are not applying for themselves (nonapplicants), but are

applying for someone else (e.g., parents who are not lawfully present applying for their U.S. citizen child) are only required to provide an SSN to an exchange under certain circumstances).

[75] CRS Report R40889, *Noncitizen Eligibility and Verification Issues in the Health Care Reform Legislation*, by Ruth Ellen Wasem.

[76] Examples of biometric identifiers include digitized photographs, finger prints, and iris scans. The biometric identifier included in U.S. passports is a digitized photograph.

[77] For a full discussion of these issues, see CRS Report RL33973, *Unauthorized Employment in the United States: Issues, Options, and Legislation*, by Andorra Bruno.

[78] For a full discussion of issues related to verification, see CRS Report R40889, *Noncitizen Eligibility and Verification Issues in the Health Care Reform Legislation*, by Ruth Ellen Wasem; and CRS Report RL33973, *Unauthorized Employment in the United States: Issues, Options, and Legislation*, by Andorra Bruno.

[79] For a full discussion of these documents, see CRS Report R40889, *Noncitizen Eligibility and Verification Issues in the Health Care Reform Legislation*, by Ruth Ellen Wasem.

[80] The United States does not require its citizens to have legal documents that verify their citizenship and identity (i.e., national identification cards). U.S. passports contain biometric identifiers (i.e., digitized photographs), as do some states' drivers licenses.

[81] For example, the Deficit Reduction Act of 2005 (P.L. 109-171), as amended, requires states to obtain satisfactory documentation of citizenship to determine eligibility for Medicaid. In a 2007 survey by the U.S. Government Accountability Office (GAO) assessing the impact of this requirement, 22 of 44 states that responded reported declines in enrollment due to the new citizenship documentation requirement. Of the 22 states reporting enrollment declines to GAO, a majority (16 states) attributed them to Medicaid coverage delays or losses of Medicaid coverage for individuals who appeared to be U.S. citizens. The extent to which the citizenship requirement is deterring ineligible noncitizens from applying for Medicaid is unknown. GAO, *States Reported That Citizenship Documentation Requirement Resulted in Enrollment Declines for Eligible Citizens and Posed Administrative Burdens*, GAO-07-889, June 2007. For a more detailed discussion of the Medicaid citizenship documentation requirements and the effects on enrollment, see CRS Report RS22629, *Medicaid Citizenship Documentation*, by Ruth Ellen Wasem.

[82] Westat, *Findings of the E-Verify Program Evaluation*, Report Prepared for the Department of Homeland Security, Rockville, MS, December 2009, p. xxxi, http://www.uscis.gov/USCIS /E-Verify/E-Verify/Final%20EVerify%20Report%2012-16-09_2.pdf. For a detailed discussion of these findings, see CRS Report R40446, *Electronic Employment Eligibility Verification*, by Andorra Bruno.

[83] U.S. Citizenship and Immigration Services, *Westat Evaluation of the E-Verify Program: USCIS Synopsis of Key Findings and Program Implications*, Washington, DC, January 28, 2010, http://www.uscis.gov/USCIS/ Native%20Docs/Westat%20Evaluation%20of%20 the%20E-Verify%20Program.pdf.

[84] For an example of this concern, see Dinah Wiley, "The Administration's New Welcome Mat for Immigrants: 'It's Safe to Apply,'" *A Children's Health Policy Blog,* Georgetown University Health Policy Institute, Center for Children and Families, October 29, 2013, http://ccf.georgetown.edu/all/the-administrations-new-welcome-mat-for-immigrantsits-safe-to-apply/.

[85] It does not matter whether the information is provided to DHS to verify immigration status or if it is provided by another source (e.g., application assistors). Immigration and Customs Enforcement, *Clarification of Existing Practices Related to Certain Health Care*

*Information*, Washington, DC, October 25, 2013, http://www.ice.gov/doclib/ero-outreach/pdf/ice-aca-memo.pdf.

[86] 45 C.F.R. §155.310(a)(2).

[87] Under the Immigration and Nationality Act (INA), aliens may be denied admission to the United States or adjustment of status if they are deemed "likely at any time to become a public charge." 8 U.S.C. §1182(a)(4)(A). In addition, any alien who, within five years after the date of entry, has become a public charge from causes that preexisted prior to entry may be removed. For a discussion of this issue, see CRS Report R41104, *Immigration Visa Issuances and Grounds for Exclusion: Policy and Trends*, by Ruth Ellen Wasem, and CRS Report R43220, *Public Charge Grounds of Inadmissibility and Deportability: Legal Overview*, by Kate M. Manuel.

[88] Center for Medicare and Medicaid Services, *What do immigrant families need to know about the Marketplace?*, Baltimore, MD, https://www.healthcare.gov/what-do-immigrant-families-need-to-know/.

[89] For a detailed discussion of S. 744, see CRS Report R43097, *Comprehensive Immigration Reform in the 113th Congress: Major Provisions in Senate-Passed S. 744*, by Ruth Ellen Wasem.

[90] Thus, U.S. citizens' unmarried sons and daughters and LPRs' unmarried sons and daughters, as well as persons who are U.S. citizens' married sons and daughters under age 31, could reside in the United States until their visa date becomes current. U.S. citizens' siblings and adult sons and daughters age 31 or older with pending family preference visas could reside in the United States for 60 days per year, but would not be authorized to work. For background on family-based admissions, see CRS Report R43145, *U.S. Family-Based Immigration Policy*, by William A. Kandel.

[91] S. 744 §4417.

[92] S. 744 §§2101, 2211(c)(4), 2309(c).

[93] For example, see Glenn Kessler, "Ted Cruz's Errant Tweet that Employers Would have a 'Huge Incentive' to Hire Newly Legalized Workers," *The Washington Post*, June 21, 2013, and Jon Feere, "Amnesty Bill No Benefit to American Workers," *The National Interest*, July 2, 2013; http://nationalinterest.org/commentary/amnesty-bill-nobenefit-american-workers .

[94] The Health Insurance Portability and Accountability Act of 1996, as amended.

[95] Section 2716 of the Public Health Service Act, as added by the ACA.

[96] For more on the employer mandate and penalty, see CRS Report R41159, *Potential Employer Penalties Under the Patient Protection and Affordable Care Act (ACA)*, by Julie M. Whittaker.

[97] Coverage is inadequate if it is defined as <60% actuarial value. Coverage is defined as unaffordable if the employee's share of premiums equal > 9.5% of household income.

[98] See also H.Res. 555, and H.Rept. 113-422.

[99] 45 C.F.R. §152.2; 75 Fed. Reg. 45029, July 30, 2010, as amended by 77 Fed. Reg. 52616, Aug. 30, 2012.

[100] 26 C.F.R. §§1.36B-1(g) (premium tax credit), 1.5000A-3(c)(2)(ii)(B) (individual mandate); 42 C.F.R. §600.5 (basic health program); 45 C.F.R. §155.20 (exchanges).

[101] PRWORA (P.L. 104-193) created the term "qualified alien," to encompass the different categories of noncitizens who were not prohibited by PRWORA from receiving federal public benefits. Qualified aliens (noted in P.L. 104-193 §431; 8 U.S.C. §1641) are defined as:

1. Legal Permanent Residents (LPRs);

2. refugees (an alien who is admitted to the United States under §207 of the Immigration and Nationality Act (INA));
3. asylees (an alien who is granted asylum under INA §208);
4. an alien who is paroled into the United States (under INA §212(d)(5)) for a period of at least one year;
5. an alien whose deportation is being withheld on the basis of prospective persecution (under INA §243(h) or §241(b)(3));
6. an alien granted conditional entry pursuant to INA §203(a)(7) as in effect prior to April 1, 1980; and
7. Cuban/Haitian entrants (as defined by P.L. 96-422).
Additionally, victims of trafficking (T-visa holders) are treated as refugees for the purpose of receiving benefits.

[102] Nonimmigrant status are defined in INA §101(a)(15), 8 U.S.C. §1101(a)(15).

[103] 8 U.S.C.§1182(d)(5).

[104] 8 U.S.C. §1160 or 1255a.

[105] INA §244, 8 U.S.C. §1254a.

[106] 8 U.S.C. §1158.

[107] 8 U.S.C. §1231.

[108] INA §101(a)(27)(J), 8 U.S.C. §1101(a)(27)(J).

[109] Data are available at http://www.census.gov/acs/www/data_documentation/2012_release/.

[110] A foreign-born person is anyone in the United States who was born in another country and did not automatically acquire U.S. citizenship at birth. For a discussion of the methodology, see CRS Report R41592, *The U.S. Foreign-Born Population: Trends and Selected Characteristics*, by William A. Kandel.

[111] Under U.S. immigration law, all legal permanent residents are potential citizens and may become so through a process known as *naturalization*. With very limited exceptions, under the law, naturalized U.S. citizens are treated the same as natural-born U.S. citizens.

[112] Since the CPS does not ask citizenship status, CRS does not use the CPS to estimate the different noncitizen populations (e.g., legal permanent residents, temporary workers, unauthorized aliens).

[113] See footnote 111.

[114] This was formerly known as the Pew Hispanic Center.

[115] The only usage of the term "unauthorized alien" in the Immigration and Nationality Act (INA) refers to noncitizens who are not authorized to work in the United States (see INA §274A). Colloquially, this term is generally used to refer to noncitizens who lack legal authorization to be present in the United States. Unauthorized aliens may have entered the United States between ports of entry, entered with false documents, or overstayed or violated the terms of their visas. This terminology is discussed in more details in the section below entitled "Definition of Lawfully Present."

[116] Part of the undercount of noncitizens comes from noncitizens reporting that they are naturalized U.S. citizens.

[117] Jeffrey S. Passel, D'Vera Cohn, and Ana Gonzalez-Barrera, *Population Decline of Unauthorized Immigrants Stalls, May Have Reversed*, Pew Hispanic Center, Washington, DC, Sept. 23, 2013, http://www.pewhispanic.org/2013/09/23/ population-decline-of-unauthorized-immigrants-stalls-may-have-reversed/.

[118] For a discussion of the differences in the methodologies of the estimates, see CRS Report RL33874, *Unauthorized Aliens Residing in the United States: Estimates Since 1986*, by Ruth Ellen Wasem.

[119] For example see, Alan Lee, *Administration Giving Quasi Legal Status to DREAMERS with Work Authorization and Possible Travel Permission,* Immigration Daily, June 15, 2012, http://www.ilw.com/articles/2012,0615-Lee.shtm; and Dean H. Judson and David A. Swanson, *Estimating Characteristics of the Foreign Born by Legal Status,* SpringerBriefs in Population Studies, 2, 2011.

[120] Jeffrey S. Passel, D'Vera Cohn, and Ana Gonzalez-Barrera, *Population Decline of Unauthorized Immigrants Stalls, May Have Reversed*, Pew Hispanic Center, Washington, DC, Sept. 23, 2013, http://www.pewhispanic.org/2013/09/23/ population-decline-of-unauthorized-immigrants-stalls-may-have-reversed/.

[121] For further background, see CRS Report RL32004, *Social Security Benefits for Noncitizens*, by Dawn Nuschler and Alison Siskin.

[122] For further background, see CRS Report RS20844, *Temporary Protected Status: Current Immigration Policy and Issues*, by Ruth Ellen Wasem and Karma Ester.

[123] For further background, see CRS Report RL32621, *U.S. Immigration Policy on Asylum Seekers*, by Ruth Ellen Wasem.

[124] For further background, see CRS Report RL32235, *U.S. Immigration Policy on Permanent Admissions*, by Ruth Ellen Wasem.

[125] The extent that some nonimmigrant (e.g., temporary workers, tourists, or foreign students) overstay their temporary visas and become "quasi-legal" aliens with petitions pending to adjust to legal status is discussed in CRS Report RS22446, *Nonimmigrant Overstays: Brief Synthesis of the Issue*, by Ruth Ellen Wasem.

[126] For further background, see CRS Report RL32621, *U.S. Immigration Policy on Asylum Seekers*, by Ruth Ellen Wasem.

[127] For a full analysis of this issue, see Citizenship and Immigration Services Ombudsman, *2007 Annual Report to Congress*, June 11, 2007.

In: The Affordable Care Act
Editor: Eileen H. Blume
ISBN: 978-1-63117-871-9


*Chapter 2*

# INDIVIDUAL MANDATE UNDER ACA*

*Annie L. Mach*

## SUMMARY

Beginning in 2014, ACA requires most individuals to maintain health insurance coverage or otherwise pay a penalty. Specifically, most individuals will be required to maintain minimum essential coverage, which is a term defined in ACA and its implementing regulations and includes most private and public coverage (e.g., employer-sponsored coverage, individual coverage, Medicare, and Medicaid, among others). Some individuals will be exempt from the mandate and the penalty, while others may receive financial assistance to help them pay for the cost of health insurance coverage and the costs associated with using health care services.

Individuals who do not maintain minimum essential coverage and are not exempt from the mandate will have to pay a penalty for each month of noncompliance with the mandate. The penalty is the greater of a flat dollar amount or a percentage of applicable income. In 2014, the annual penalty is the greater of $95 or 1% of applicable income; the penalty increases in 2015 and 2016 and is adjusted for inflation thereafter. The penalty will be collected through federal income tax returns. The Internal Revenue Service (IRS) can attempt to collect any owed penalties by reducing the amount of an individual's tax refund;

* This is an edited, reformatted and augmented version of a Congressional Research Service publication R41331, prepared for Members and Committees of Congress, dated May 5, 2014.

however, individuals who fail to pay the penalty will not be subject to any criminal prosecution or penalty for such failure. The Secretary of the Treasury cannot file notice of lien or file a levy on any property for a taxpayer who does not pay the penalty.

Certain individuals will be exempt from the individual mandate and the penalty. For example, individuals with qualifying religious exemptions and those whose household income is below the filing threshold for federal income taxes will not be subject to the penalty. ACA allows the Secretary of Health and Human Services (HHS) to grant hardship exemptions from the penalty to anyone determined to have suffered a hardship with respect to the capability to obtain coverage. The Secretary of HHS has identified a number of different circumstances that would allow individuals to receive a hardship exemption, including an individual not being eligible for Medicaid based on a state's decision not to carry out the ACA expansion and financial or domestic circumstances that prevent an individual from obtaining coverage (e.g., eviction or recent experience of domestic violence).

ACA includes several reporting requirements designed, in part, to assist individuals in providing evidence of having met the mandate. Every person (including employers, insurers, and government programs) that provides minimum essential coverage to any individual must provide a return to the IRS that includes information about the individual's health insurance coverage.

On March 5, 2014, the House of Representatives passed H.R. 4118, Suspending the Individual Mandate Penalty Law Equals (SIMPLE) Fairness Act. H.R. 4118 provides that individuals do not have to pay an individual mandate penalty for any month prior to January 1, 2015, effectively delaying implementation of the individual mandate penalty and maintaining the initial penalty levels until 2015.

This report describes the individual mandate as established under the Affordable Care Act (ACA, P.L. 111-148, as amended).[1] The report also discusses the ACA reporting requirements designed, in part, to assist individuals in providing evidence of having met the mandate.

## Individual Mandate

Beginning in 2014, ACA requires most individuals to have health insurance coverage or potentially pay a penalty for noncompliance.[2] Individuals will be required to maintain minimum essential coverage for themselves and their dependents. Some individuals will be exempt from the mandate and the penalty, while others may receive financial assistance to help them pay for the cost of health insurance coverage and the costs associated with using health care services.

## Minimum Essential Coverage

In general, individuals who are not exempt from the mandate must maintain minimum essential coverage to avoid the penalty. Minimum essential coverage is defined broadly in statute and is further defined in regulations; the definition includes most types of government-sponsored coverage (e.g., Medicare) as well as most types of private insurance (e.g., employer-sponsored insurance). *Table A-1* provides detailed information about how different types of health insurance coverage relate to the definition of minimum essential coverage and the penalty. Minimum essential coverage does not include health insurance coverage consisting of excepted benefits, such as dental-only coverage.

## Penalty

With some exceptions, individuals will be required to maintain minimum essential coverage for themselves and their dependents.[3] Those who do not meet the mandate may be required to pay a penalty for each month of noncompliance. The penalty will be calculated as the *greater* of either:

1) a percentage of the "applicable income," defined as the amount by which an individual's household income exceeds the applicable filing threshold for the applicable tax year.[4] The filing threshold comprises the personal exemption amount (doubled for those married filing jointly) plus the standard deduction amount,[5]
    - the percentage will be 1.0% in 2014, 2.0% in 2015, and 2.5% thereafter, or
2) a flat dollar amount assessed on each taxpayer and any dependents (e.g., family)
    - the annual flat dollar amount phased in—$95 in 2014, $325 in 2015, and $695 in 2016 and beyond (adjusted for inflation),[6] assessed for each taxpayer and any dependents;

- the amount is reduced by one-half for dependents under the age of 18;
- the total family penalty is capped at 300% of the annual flat dollar amount.

The penalty for noncompliance cannot exceed the national average premium for bronze-levelqualified health plans offered through exchanges (for the relevant family size).[7] Any penalty that taxpayers are required to pay for themselves or their dependents must be included in their return for the taxable year. Those individuals who file joint returns are jointly liable for the penalty.

### Illustrative Individual Mandate Penalties

The following examples illustrate the penalty for a single individual and for a family of four. Penalty amounts are shown for 2014, 2015, and 2016. To summarize the penalty (as described above) for those individuals whose household income is above the filing threshold amount for federal income tax, the penalty is the greater of a flat dollar amount or a percentage of applicable income (income above the filing threshold). Individuals below the filing threshold for federal income tax will not pay a penalty.

In the 2014 examples, the 2014 filing threshold is used, which is $10,150 for a single individual under age 65 with no dependents (single filing status) and $20,300 for a married couple filing jointly. The filing thresholds for 2015 and 2016 have not yet been determined, but because they are linked to an inflation adjustment based on the CPI-U,[8] they will likely be higher when implemented in 2015 and 2016. The examples below use estimated filing thresholds for 2015 and 2016.[9] As a result, the numbers for 2015 and 2016 are meant for illustrative purposes only. These examples are best used to show the relative scope of the penalties and the relationship between the various components of the formulas for calculating the penalty.

Illustrative individual mandate penalties for a single individual with no dependents:

- In 2014, those with income above the filing threshold ($10,150 in 2014) but at or below $19,650 will pay the $95 flat amount, those with income above $19,650 and below the cap at the national average premium for bronze-level coverage will pay 1% of applicable income;
- In 2015, those with income above the filing threshold (estimated to be $10,300 in 2015) but at or below an estimated $26,550 will pay the $325 flat amount, and those with income above an estimated $26,550

and below the cap at the national average premium for bronze-level coverage will pay 2% of applicable income;

- In 2016, those with income above the filing threshold (estimated to be $10,450 in 2016) but at or below an estimated $38,250 will pay the $695 flat amount, and those with income above an estimated $38,250 and below the cap at the national average premium for bronze-level coverage will pay 2.5% of applicable income.

In calculating the penalty for a family, each of the components of the formula increases for a family, including the filing threshold, flat dollar amount, and the cost of a bronze-level plan. However, the flat dollar amount for a family cannot be greater than three times the amount for an individual. For example, in 2014 the flat dollar amount is limited to three times $95, or $285. The flat dollar amount is one-half for children under 18, so that a married couple with two children under 18, a single parent with four children under 18, as well as larger families are all subject to the same flat dollar maximum amount. However, these families may still pay larger penalties, if they have higher incomes.

Illustrative individual mandate penalties for a family of four (married couple with two children under age 18):

- In 2014, those with income above the filing threshold ($20,300 in 2014) but at or below $48,800 will pay the $285 flat dollar amount, those with income above $48,800 and below the cap at the national average premium for bronze-level family coverage will pay 1% of applicable income;
- In 2015, those with income above the filing threshold (estimated to be $20,600 in 2015) but at or below an estimated $69,350 will pay the $975 flat dollar amount, those with income above an estimated $69,350 and below the cap at the national average premium for bronze-level family coverage will pay 2% of applicable income;

In 2016, those with income above the filing threshold (estimated to be $20,900 in 2016) but at or below an estimated $104,300 will pay the $2,085 flat dollar amount, those with income above an estimated $104,300 and below the cap at the national average premium for bronze-level family coverage will pay 2.5% of applicable income.

## Exemptions

Certain individuals (and their dependents) may be exempt from the penalty. These individuals include those whose household income is less than the filing threshold for federal income taxes for the applicable tax year (filing threshold exemption), as well as those whose required contribution for self-only coverage[10] for a calendar year exceeds 8% of household income (affordability exemption).[11] After 2014, this percentage will be adjusted to reflect the excess rate of premium growth above the rate of income growth for the period.

Certain categories of individuals will be exempt from the individual mandate, including those with qualifying religious exemptions,[12] those in a health care sharing ministry,[13] individuals not lawfully present in the United States, and incarcerated individuals (except those pending the disposition of charges). No penalty will be imposed on those without coverage for less than three months[14] or members of Indian tribes.[15] Qualifying individuals who would otherwise be subject to the mandate, but who live abroad for at least 330 days within a 12-month period, as well as bona fide residents of any possession of the United States will be considered to have minimum essential coverage and therefore not be subject to the penalty. Any individual whom the Secretary of Health and Human Services (HHS) determines to have suffered a hardship with respect to the capability to obtain coverage under a qualified health plan will be exempt (see the text box for more information about the hardship exemption).

The Internal Revenue Service (IRS) issued guidance that provides "transitional relief" from the penalty for individuals (and any dependents) who were eligible for non-calendar year employer-sponsored insurance plans in 2013.[16] For example, consider an individual who was eligible to enroll in his/her employer's health plan, whose plan year began on September 1, 2013, and ends on August 31, 2014. Under the transitional relief, the individual is not liable for the individual mandate penalty for January 2014 through August 2014, as the individual would have had to enroll in the employer-sponsored plan in 2013 in order to be covered by the plan in those months of 2014.

Additionally, the IRS has issued guidance that provides that individuals enrolled in certain types of coverage that are not considered minimum essential coverage will not be liable for a penalty.[17] For example, women who only receive pregnancy-related services under Medicaid do not have minimum essential coverage, but IRS indicates that these women will not be liable for a penalty in 2014. These "exemptions" from the penalty are not discussed in the

"Claiming an Exemption" section of this report; however, they are identified in *Table A-1* in the Appendix of this report.

**Hardship Exemption**

Any individual whom the Secretary of HHS determines has suffered a hardship with respect to the capability to obtain health insurance coverage will receive a hardship exemption. Through regulations and guidance, HHS has identified a number of circumstances that would allow individuals to receive a hardship exemption:[18]

1) an individual experiences financial, domestic, or other circumstances that prevent him/her from obtaining coverage or the expense of purchasing coverage would have caused him/her to experience serious deprivation of food, shelter, clothing, or other necessities;[19]
2) an individual is unable to afford coverage based on projected household income;
3) an individual whose income is below the filing threshold (and therefore eligible for the filing threshold exemption), except that the individual claimed a dependent with a filing requirement and had household income exceeding the filing threshold as a result;
4) an individual is ineligible for Medicaid based on a state's decision not to carry out the ACA expansion;
5) an individual is identified eligible for affordable self-only employer-sponsored insurance (ESI), but the aggregate cost of the ESI for all the employed members of the family exceeds 8% of household income;
6) an individual is an Indian eligible for services through an Indian health care provider, but is not eligible for an exemption based on being a member of an Indian tribe, or is eligible for services through the Indian Health Service;
7) an individual who enrolls in a plan offered through an exchange or the State Children's Health Insurance Program (CHIP) prior to the close of the open enrollment period (March 31, 2014) will be able to claim a hardship exemption for the months prior to the effective date of the individual's coverage;[20] or
8) an individual has been notified that his/her plan will not be renewed and believes that the available plan options are more expensive than the plan that was not renewed.[21]

Individuals who claim hardship exemptions are eligible to purchase catastrophic plans. Under ACA, catastrophic plans must cover a comprehensive set of benefits, but they do not have to comply with the same cost-sharing requirements with which other plans must comply under ACA. As a result, these plans typically have lower premiums because they have higher cost-sharing. Only individuals who are either under age 30 or eligible for a hardship or affordability exemption from the individual mandate are eligible to enroll in catastrophic plans.[22]

## Claiming an Exemption

Individuals can be exempt from the mandate and the penalty based on an individual's characteristics, financial status, or affiliations (e.g., religious affiliations). Some individuals who are exempt will not be expected to take any actions to claim the exemption; others will have to either obtain a certification of exemption from a health insurance exchange or claim the exemption through the tax filing process.

Individuals who live abroad for more than 330 days in a 12-month period and those who are bona fide residents of a U.S. possession do not have to take any action to claim the exemption. Those claiming the short coverage gap, unlawfully present, filing threshold, or affordability exemptions may only do so on their federal income tax return. In order to claim a religious exemption an individual must obtain an exemption certification issued by the exchange serving the area in which the individual resides. Some types of hardship exemptions can be claimed by receiving a certification from an exchange, while other types can only be claimed through the tax filing process.[23] All other exemptions may be certified by an exchange *or* may be claimed on the filer's federal income tax return.[24]

Regulations provide that most exemptions be applicable retrospectively (with an exception for a specific hardship definition) and be recertified annually; only the religious and Indian tribe exemptions are eligible for prospective or retrospective applicability and continuous certification. *Table 1* outlines the basic features of the nine exemption categories.

**Table 1. Individual Mandate Exemptions under ACA**

| Exemption | Eligibility Certification | Applicability | Recertification |
|---|---|---|---|
| Religious conscience | Exchange only | Prospective or retrospective | Continuous[a] |
| Hardship | Exchange or tax filing | Retrospective[b] | Annual |
| Health care sharing ministry membership | Exchange or tax filing | Retrospective | Annual |
| Indian tribe membership | Exchange or tax filing | Prospective or retrospective | Continuous |
| Incarceration | Exchange or tax filing | Retrospective | Annual |
| Affordability | Tax filing only | Retrospective | Annual |
| Unlawful resident | Tax filing only | Retrospective | Annual |
| Coverage gap | Tax filing only | Retrospective | Annual |
| Filing threshold | Not applicable[c] | Retrospective | Annual |

Sources: 45 C.F.R. Part 155 and 26 C.F.R. Part 1.

Note: The "exemptions" for qualifying individuals who live abroad for at least 330 days within a 12 month period and bona fide residents of any possession of the United States are not included in this table because individuals who meet one of these criteria do not need to take any action to comply with the individual mandate.

[a] Reapplication for the exemption is required when an individual reaches age 21. See 45 C.F.R. §155.605(c).

[b] One type of hardship exemption is available prospectively; it is available to individuals for whom qualifying coverage is unaffordable based on projected income.

[c] Individuals who qualify for a filing threshold exemption are not required to file a tax return or apply to an exchange to claim the exemption; these individuals are automatically exempt and do not need to take further action to secure an exemption. However, if the individuals choose to file a return they may claim the exemption on the return.

## Failure to Pay Penalty

Taxpayers who are required to pay a penalty but fail to do so will receive a notice from IRS stating that they owe the penalty. If they still do not pay the penalty, the IRS can attempt to collect the funds by reducing the amount of their tax refund for that year or future years. However, individuals who fail to pay the penalty will not be subject to any criminal prosecution or penalty for such failure. The Secretary of the Treasury cannot file notice of lien or file a levy on any property for a taxpayer who does not pay the penalty.

# POTENTIAL FINANCIAL ASSISTANCE

While ACA requires most individuals to maintain minimum essential coverage, it provides financial assistance to some individuals to help them meet the requirement. Under the ACA Medicaid expansion, some states have expanded their Medicaid programs to include all nonelderly, non-pregnant individuals with income below 133% of the federal poverty level (FPL), which is expected to significantly increase Medicaid enrollment.[25] Beginning in 2014, some individuals who do not qualify for Medicaid coverage, but who meet other ACA requirements, will be provided with subsidies to help pay for the premiums and cost-sharing requirements of health plans offered through an exchange.[26]

# REPORTING MINIMUM ESSENTIAL COVERAGE

ACA requires that information be provided to the IRS and to individuals, in part to ensure that they have both knowledge and proof of meeting the individual mandate.[27] Every person (including employers, insurers, and government programs) that provides minimum essential coverage to any individual must provide a return to the IRS and a statement to the covered individual.

The person required to provide the return and statement is referred to as the "reporting entity." In general, insurers are the reporting entities for all fully insured health insurance arrangements, and plan sponsors are the reporting entities for all self-insured arrangements.[28] A government agency or unit is the reporting entity for any coverage under a government-sponsored program, including any coverage that is provided through an insurer (e.g., a Medicare Advantage plan). An insurer does not have to provide a return or a statement for any coverage it offers through an individual health insurance exchange, as the exchange is the reporting entity for such coverage; however, insurers that offer small group coverage through a small business health options program (SHOP) exchange are the reporting entities for such coverage.

The return provided to the IRS must include the following:

- the name, address, and employer identification number (EIN) of the reporting entity required to file the return;
- the name, address, and taxpayer identification number (TIN) of the "responsible individual"[29] and each other individual covered under the policy or program;[30]
- the months for which, for at least one day, each individual was covered under the policy or program;
- for coverage provided through the group plan of an employer—
- the name, address, and EIN of the employer sponsoring the plan;
- whether the coverage is a qualified health plan (QHP) offered through a SHOP exchange and the SHOP's unique identifier;
- and any other information as specified in forms, instructions, or published guidance issued by the Department of the Treasury.

The reporting entity is also responsible for providing a statement to each responsible individual covered under the policy or program. The statement must include the contact information for the person designated as the reporting entity's contact person; the policy number of the coverage, if any; and the information included in the return to the IRS for the responsible individual and any individuals listed on the return.

Reporting entities were required to begin submitting returns in 2014; however, in July 2013 the Department of Treasury published a notice that delayed the reporting requirement until 2015.[31] Reporting entities that do not file timely and accurate returns and those that do not provide statements to individuals could be subject to penalties.

# Appendix A. Health Insurance Coverage and the Individual Mandate

### Table A-1. Types of Health Insurance Coverage as they Relate to the Definition of Minimum Essential Coverage and the Individual Mandate Penalty in 2014

| Type of Coverage | Is it considered minimum essential coverage in 2014? | If it is an individual's only source of coverage in 2014, is the individual liable for the individual mandate penalty? |
|---|---|---|
| Medicare Part A | Yes | No |

**Table A-1. (Continued)**

| Type of Coverage | Is it considered minimum essential coverage in 2014? | If it is an individual's only source of coverage in 2014, is the individual liable for the individual mandate penalty? |
|---|---|---|
| Medicare Advantage | Yes | No |
| Medicaid full benefit coverage | Yes | No |
| Medicaid limited benefit coverage | | |
| Optional coverage of family planning servicesa | No | No |
| Optional coverage of tuberculosis-related servicesb | No | No |
| Coverage of pregnancy-related services[c] | No | No |
| Coverage limited to treatment of emergency medical conditions[d] | No | No |
| Coverage authorized under §1115(a)(2) of the Social Security Act (SSA)[e] | According to a proposed rule issued by the Internal Revenue Service (IRS), this coverage is not considered minimum essential coverage[f] | No |
| Medicaid coverage for the medically needy[g] | According to a proposed rule issued by the IRS, this coverage is not considered minimum essential coverage[f] | No |
| State Children's Health Insurance Program (CHIP) TRICARE | Yes | No |
| Limited benefit TRICARE programs[h] | According to a proposed rule issued by the IRS, this coverage is not considered minimum essential coverage[f] | No |
| Other coverage offered under TRICARE | Yes | No |
| VA Health Care Programs[i] Medical benefits package authorized for eligible veterans under 38 U.S.C. 1710 and 38 U.S.C. 1705 | Yes | No |
| Civilian Health and Medical | Yes | No |

| Type of Coverage | Is it considered minimum essential coverage in 2014? | If it is an individual's only source of coverage in 2014, is the individual liable for the individual mandate penalty? |
|---|---|---|
| Program of the Department of Veterans Affairs (CHAMPVA) authorized under 38 U.S.C. 1781[j] | | |
| Comprehensive health care program authorized under 38 U S.C. 1803 and 38 U.S.C. 1821 for certain children of Vietnam Veterans and Veterans of covered service in Korea who are suffering spina bifida | Yes | No |
| Peace Corps Program Nonappropriated Fund | Yes | No |
| Health Benefits Program of the Department of Defense | Yes | No |
| Employer-sponsored health insurance | Yes | No |
| Individual market health insurance | Yes | No |
| Qualified health plans | | |
| (QHP) offered inside and outside exchanges | Yes | No |
| Grandfathered health plans[k] | Yes | No |
| Self-funded student health plans[l] | Yes | No |
| Refugee Medical Assistance supported by the Administration for Children and Families | Yes | No |
| State high risk pools[m] | Yes | No |
| Group health plan provided through insurance regulated by a foreign government | Yes[n] | No |

Source: CRS analysis of ACA statute, 26 C.F.R. Part 1, and its implementing regulations and guidance.

Notes: ACA allows the Secretary of HHS, in coordination with the Secretary of the Treasury, to recognize arrangements other than those identified in statute as minimum essential coverage. HHS has outlined a procedure by which a sponsor of coverage or a government agency may apply to HHS to have its coverage certified as minimum essential coverage. The process is outlined in 45 C.F.R. §156.604 and in guidance issued by HHS, CCIIO Sub-Regulatory Guidance: Process for Obtaining Recognition as Minimum Essential Coverage, on October 31, 2013.

[a] As defined in 42 U.S.C. 1396a(a)(10)(A)(ii)(XXI).

[b] As defined in 42 U.S.C. 1396a(a)(10)(A)(ii)(XII).

[c] As defined in 42 U.S.C. 1396a(a)(10)(A)(i)(V) and 1396a(a)(10)(A)(ii)(IX).

[d] As authorized by 42 U.S.C. 1396b(v).

[e] In general, §1115 of the Social Security Act (SSA) gives the Secretary of HHS authority to approve experimental, pilot, or demonstration projects that promote the objectives of the Medicaid and CHIP programs. Section 1115(a)(2) of the SSA allows a state to extend benefits to additional populations (expansion populations) that would not otherwise be eligible for Medicaid. The coverage a state extends to expansion populations is not required to be comprehensive and may be limited.

[f] While generally not considered minimum essential coverage, to the extent such coverage is comprehensive coverage, the Secretaries of HHS and the Treasury may recognize such coverage as minimum essential coverage. See the proposed rule for more details (78 *Federal Register* 4302, January 27, 2014).

[g] As defined in 42 U.S.C. 1396a(a)(10)(C) and 42 C.F.R. 435.300 and following (Subpart D).

[h] Specifically, the program providing care limited to the space available in a facility for the uniformed services for individuals excluded from TRICARE coverage under sections 1079(a), 1086(c)(1), or 1086(d)(1) of Title 10, U.S.C., and the program for individuals not on active duty for an injury, illness, or disease, incurred or aggravated in the line of duty under sections 1074a and 1074b of Title 10, U.S.C.

[i] P.L. 111-173 amended ACA to clarify that the Secretary of Veterans Affairs, in coordination with the Secretary of HHS and the Secretary of the Treasury, would determine which VA health care programs would be considered minimum essential coverage. The programs outlined in the table are the VA programs the Secretaries have identified as minimum essential coverage; it would seem that coverage under any VA programs other than those specified in the table is not considered minimum essential coverage. For more information on VA health care under ACA, see CRS Report R41198, *TRICARE and VA Health Care: Impact of the Patient Protection and Affordable Care Act (ACA)*, by Sidath Viranga Panangala and Don J. Jansen.

[g] For more information on the Civilian Health and Medical Program of the Department of Veterans Affairs (CHAMPVA), see CRS Report RS22483, *Health Care for Dependents and Survivors of Veterans*, by Sidath Viranga Panangala.

[k] Grandfathered plans are defined as those individual and group plans that an individual or family was enrolled in on the date of enactment (March 23, 2010). For additional information about grandfathered plans, see CRS Report R41166, *Grandfathered Health Plans Under the Patient Protection and Affordable Care Act (ACA)*, by Bernadette Fernandez.

[l] Self-funded student health plans are designated minimum essential coverage for plan or policy years beginning on or before December 31, 2014; for coverage beginning after December 31, 2014, sponsors of such plans have to apply to the Secretary of HHS to be recognized as minimum essential coverage via the process outlined in 45 C.F.R. §156.604.

[m] State high risk pools are designated as minimum essential coverage for plan or policy years beginning on or before December 31, 2014; for coverage beginning after December 31, 2014, sponsors of high risk pool coverage have to apply to the Secretary of HHS to be recognized as minimum essential coverage via the process outlined in 45 C.F.R. §156.604.

[n] According to guidance from HHS, an individual who has coverage under a group health plan provided through insurance regulated by a foreign government has minimum essential coverage if the individual is "physically absent from the United States ..." and if the individual is "physically present in the United States ... while the individual is on expatriate status." For more information see *CCIIO Sub-Regulatory Guidance: Process for Obtaining Recognition as Minimum Essential Coverage*, issued October 31, 2013.

## End Notes

[1] On June 28, 2012, the U.S. Supreme Court issued its decision in National Federation of Independent Business v. Sebelius, finding that the individual mandate in Section 5000A of the Internal Revenue Code (as added by §1501 of ACA), is a constitutional exercise of Congress's authority to levy taxes. However, the Court held that it was not a valid exercise of Congress's power under the Commerce Clause or the Necessary and Proper Clause. For more information, see CRS Report WSLG112, Supreme Court Upholds the Individual Mandate as a Permissible Exercise of Congress' Taxing Power, by Erika K. Lunder.

[2] §1501(b) as amended by §10106 (b) of P.L. 111-148 and by §1002 of P.L. 111-152 adds Chapter 49, Maintenance of Essential Coverage, to Subtitle D of the Internal Revenue Code of 1986.

[3] In the final rule on maintaining minimum essential coverage (78 FR 53646, August 30, 2013), IRS provides that a taxpayer is liable for an individual mandate penalty for his/her dependents regardless of whether the taxpayer claims the dependents for the taxable year. For the purposes of this provision, "dependent" is defined in §152 of the Internal Revenue Code (IRC) and includes qualifying children and qualifying relatives.

[4] Household income is defined as the modified adjusted gross income (MAGI) of the taxpayer, plus the aggregate MAGI of all other individuals for whom the taxpayer is allowed a deduction for personal exemptions for the taxable year. Modified adjusted gross income is defined as adjusted gross income increased by foreign earned income (§911 of the IRC) and any amount of tax-exempt interest received or accrued by the taxpayer during the taxable year.

[5] In 2014, the standard deduction is $6,200 and the personal exemption is $3,950, so that generally, the filing thresholds for individuals under age 65 are $10,150 for a single filing

status and $20,300 for a married couple filing jointly. The filing threshold is linked to an inflation adjustment based on the CPI-U, and therefore it may be higher in 2015 and 2016.

[6] The inflation adjustment will be based on the cost-of-living adjustment (CPI-U), for the calendar year, with any increase that is not a multiple of $50 rounded to the next lowest multiple of $50.

[7] As of the date of this report, no information has been released as to the national average premiums of bronze-level plans offered through exchanges.

[8] The Consumer Price Index for all Urban Consumers (CPI-U) is a measure of inflation published by the U.S. Bureau of Labor Statistics. One way in which it is used is to calculate annual inflation adjustments to personal income tax brackets.

[9] The estimated filing thresholds for 2015 and 2016 are not based on the formula IRS uses to adjust the filing thresholds; rather, they were calculated using the Congressional Budget Office's CPI-U forecast for 2015 and 2016 and then rounding down the estimates to the nearest $50. The Congressional Budget Office's CPI-U forecast was obtained from The Budget and Economic Outlook: 2014 to 2024, http://www.cbo.gov/sites/default/files/cbofiles/attachments/45010-Outlook2014_Feb.pdf.

[10] Required contribution is defined as (1) in the case of an individual eligible to purchase minimum essential coverage through an employer (other than through the exchange), the portion of the annual premium that is paid by the individual for self-only coverage, or (2) for individuals not included above, the annual premium for the lowest cost bronze plan available in the individual market through the exchange in the state in which the individual resides, reduced by the amount of the premium credit for the taxable year.

[11] Household income is defined as the modified adjusted gross income (MAGI) of the taxpayer, plus the aggregate MAGI of all other individuals for whom the taxpayer is allowed a deduction for personal exemptions for the taxable year. Modified adjusted gross income is defined as adjusted gross income increased by foreign earned income (Section 911 of the IRC) and any amount of tax-exempt interest received or accrued by the taxpayer during the taxable year.

[12] In order to qualify for the religious exemption, an individual must be a member of a recognized religious sect or division (as described in 1402(g)(1) of the Internal Revenue Code of 1986) by reason of which he or she is conscientiously opposed to acceptance of the benefits of any private or public insurance that makes payments in the event of death, disability, old-age, or retirement or makes payments toward the cost of, or provides services for, medical care (including the benefits of any insurance system established by the Social Security Act, such as Social Security benefits and Medicare). Such sect or division must have been in existence at all times since December 31, 1950. There is no list of specific religious groups that qualify for the exemption. For more information, see CRS Report RL34708, Religious Exemptions for Mandatory Health Care Programs: A Legal Analysis, by Cynthia Brougher.

[13] A health care sharing ministry is defined as an organization described in Section 501(c) of the IRC (including corporations, and any community chest, fund, or foundation, organized and operated exclusively for religious, charitable, scientific, or testing for public safety) and is exempt from taxation under Section 501(a). Members of the ministry share a common set of ethical or religious beliefs and share medical expenses, and retain membership even after they develop a medical condition. The health sharing ministry must have been in existence (and sharing medical expenses) at all time since December 31, 1999, and must conduct an annual audit by an independent certified public accountant, available to the public upon request.

[14] This exemption only applies to the first short coverage gap in a calendar year.

[15] The term "Indian tribe" means any Indian tribe, band, nation, pueblo, or other organized group or community, including any Alaska Native village, or regional or village corporation, as defined in, or established pursuant to, the Alaska Native Claims Settlement Act (43 U.S.C. 1601 et seq.), that is recognized as eligible for the special programs and services provided by the United States to Indians because of their status as Indians.

[16] IRS Notice 2013-42.

[17] IRS Notice 2014-10.

[18] 45 C F.R. §155.605(g) and the guidance noted.

[19] HHS provides further guidance on these circumstances in "Guidance on Hardship Exemption Criteria and Special Enrollment Periods" published June 26, 2013, available at http://www.cms.gov/CCIIO/Resources/Regulations-andGuidance/Downloads/exemptions-guidance-6-26-2013.pdf.

[20] These circumstances are not described in regulations; the exchange aspect is described in guidance published October 28, 2013, available at http://www.cms.gov/CCIIO/Resources/Fact-Sheets-and-FAQs/Downloads/enrollmentperiod-faq-10-28-2013.pdf, and the CHIP aspect is described in guidance published March 31, 2014, available at http://www.cms.gov/CCIIO/Resources/Regulations-and-Guidance/Downloads/shared-responsibility-FAQ-3-30-2014.pdf.

[21] This circumstance is not described in regulations; it is described in guidance published December 19, 2013, available at http://www.cms.gov/CCIIO/Resources/Regulations-and-Guidance/Downloads/cancellation-consumer-options-12-19- 2013.pdf.

[22] For more information about catastrophic plans, see CRS Report R43233, Private Health Plans Under the ACA: In Brief, by Bernadette Fernandez and Annie L. Mach.

[23] Several different types of hardship exemptions are described in regulations and guidance (see the text box in this report); at least three of the types will be provided exclusively through the tax filing process, not through exchanges.

[24] According to regulations (45 C.F.R. §155.610(h)), exchanges may only certify exemptions for applications made within the calendar year for which the exemption is being sought. Individuals seeking to claim exemptions after December 31st of the relevant year must do so on their federal tax return.

[25] Originally, the assumption was that all states would implement the ACA Medicaid expansion in 2014 as required in statute because implementing the ACA Medicaid expansion was required in order for states to receive any federal Medicaid funding. However, on June 28, 2012, the U.S. Supreme Court issued its decision in National Federation of Independent Business v. Sebelius, finding that the federal government cannot terminate the federal Medicaid funding states are receiving for their current Medicaid program if a state refuses to implement the ACA Medicaid expansion. This decision effectively made the ACA Medicaid expansion optional for states. For more information, see CRS Report R43357, Medicaid: An Overview, coordinated by Alison Mitchell.

[26] For more information on premium credits and cost-sharing subsidies, see CRS Report R41137, Health Insurance Premium Credits in the Patient Protection and Affordable Care Act (ACA), by Bernadette Fernandez.

[27] 26 IRC §6055.

[28] A fully insured plan is one in which the plan sponsor purchases health coverage and the carrier assumes the risk of providing health benefits to the sponsor's enrolled members. A self-insured plan is one in which an entity (e.g., employer or association) provides coverage for its members directly by setting aside funds and paying for health benefits.

[29] In regulations, the term responsible individual includes, "a primary insured, employee, former employee, uniformed services sponsor, parent, or other related person named on an application who enrolls one more individuals, including him or herself, in minimum essential coverage." 26 C.F.R. §1.6055-1(b)(11).

[30] Regulations provide that a reporting entity is required to make a reasonable effort to obtain the TIN of each individual covered under the plan, but if a TIN is not available, the reporting entity must provide a date of birth for the individual instead.

[31] IRS Notice 2013-45.

In: The Affordable Care Act
Editor: Eileen H. Blume
ISBN: 978-1-63117-871-9


*Chapter 3*

# IMPLEMENTING THE AFFORDABLE CARE ACT: DELAYS, EXTENSIONS, AND OTHER ACTIONS TAKEN BY THE ADMINISTRATION*

***C. Stephen Redhead and Janet Kinzer***

## INTRODUCTION

The two federal agencies primarily responsible for administering the private health insurance provisions in the Patient Protection and Affordable Care Act (ACA)—the Centers for Medicare & Medicaid Services (CMS) within the Department of Health and Human Services (HHS), and the Internal Revenue Service (IRS) within the Treasury Department—have taken certain actions to delay, extend, or otherwise modify the law's implementation.[1]

*Table 1* summarizes selected administrative actions taken by CMS and the IRS to address ACA implementation. The table entries, which are grouped under general topic headings, are not organized in any particular priority order. Each entry includes a brief summary of the action and some accompanying explanatory material and comments to help provide additional context. Where available, links are provided to relevant regulatory and guidance documents

* This is an edited, reformatted and augmented version of a Congressional Research Service publication R43474, prepared for Members and Committees of Congress, dated April 14, 2014.

online. Readers are encouraged to review these documents for more details about each action taken.

The actions summarized in the table, which address some of the ACA's core insurance expansion provisions,[2] are not the result of a single policy decision. They represent multiple separate decisions taken by the Administration to address a variety of factors affecting the implementation of specific provisions of the law. In compiling the table, CRS made decisions about which administrative actions to include, and which ones to leave out. Generally, CRS included the more significant actions that have been the subject of debate among health policy analysts and, in some instances, the target of criticism by opponents of the ACA. The table is not intended to be a comprehensive list of ACA-related administrative actions.

Perhaps the most controversial action is the Administration's decision to delay enforcement of the ACA's "employer mandate." On July 9, 2013, the IRS announced that it would not take enforcement action against employers who fail to comply with the law's employer mandate until the beginning of 2015. This ACA provision, which took effect on January 1, 2014, requires employers with 50 or more full-time equivalent employees to offer their full-time workers affordable health coverage or pay a penalty if one or more employees purchase coverage through an exchange and receive a premium tax credit. The IRS subsequently announced that employers with at least 50 but fewer than 100 full-time equivalent employees will have an additional year to comply with the employer mandate. According to the Administration, these actions were taken after it concluded that the ACA's employer mandate could not be enforced until the related requirement that employers report the coverage they offer to their employees had been fully implemented. The IRS says that it is working with stakeholders to simplify the reporting process consistent with effective implementation of the law.[3]

Other controversial administrative actions include those taken in response to the decision by insurers to cancel individual and small-group health plans that do not meet the ACA's new standards for health insurance coverage, which also took effect on January 1, 2014. On November 14, 2013, the Administration notified state insurance commissioners of the option to delay enforcement of certain health insurance reforms under the ACA. It encouraged state officials to permit insurers to renew noncompliant policies in the individual and small-group market for policy years starting between January 1, 2104, and October 1, 2014.[4] The Administration has since extended this policy for two years. Thus, at the option of state regulators, insurers may continue to renew noncompliant policies at any time through October 1, 2016.[5]

Finally, HHS has been criticized for providing special enrollment periods for individuals who were unable to enroll in a qualified health plan (QHP) offered through a federally facilitated exchange prior to the March 31, 2014, deadline due to technical problems or other exceptional circumstances.[6]

Opponents of the ACA, who believe that the law is fundamentally flawed, argue that some of the Administration's actions effectively rewrite the law in an effort to make it work and confuse the public. The ACA's critics also assert that the actions taken by the Administration to delay enforcement of the employer mandate are illegal and raise concerns that the President is not upholding his constitutional duty to faithfully execute federal law.[7]

The Administration counters that its actions are not a refusal to implement and enforce the ACA as written. Instead, they represent temporary corrections necessary to ensure the effective implementation of a very large and complex law. Agency officials point to a number of factors that have made it difficult to meet various ACA deadlines. Those factors include a lack of appropriations to help fund implementation activities, technological problems including the poorly managed launch of the websites for the federally facilitated exchange and the state-based exchanges, and the need to phase in the various interconnected parts of the law so as to avoid unnecessary disruption of employment and insurance markets.[8]

Regarding the employer mandate delay, the Administration says that its actions are no different from those taken by previous administrations faced with the challenges of implementing a complicated law. The Administration notes that its decision to grant employers "transition relief," taken pursuant to administrative authority under the Internal Revenue Code to "prescribe all needful rules and regulations" to administer tax laws,[9] is part of an established practice to provide relief to taxpayers who might otherwise struggle to comply with new tax law.[10]

Notwithstanding the Administration's arguments, critics question whether some of the recent delays of ACA provisions exceed the executive's traditional discretion in enforcing law to the point that they represent a blatant disregard of the law. For example, they argue that the decision to encourage states to allow insurers to renew noncompliant policies for people who want to keep their current plans directly contravenes provisions of the ACA that had become politically inconvenient.[11]

A companion CRS report summarizes all the *legislative* actions taken by Congress since the ACA's enactment to repeal, defund, delay, or otherwise amend the law.[12]

**Table 1. Selected Administrative Delays and Other Changes to ACA Implementation**

| Summary of Administrative Action | Explanatory Notes and Comments |
|---|---|
| 2014 Open Enrollment: Hardship Exemption, December 2013 Enrollees<br>On October 28, 2013, CMS announced that it would exempt from the individual mandate penalty those individuals who wait until after February 15, 2014, to enroll in a qualified health plan (QHP) offered through an exchange during the 2014 open enrollment period. See http://www.cms.gov/CCIIO/Resources/Fact-Sheets-and-FAQs/Downloads/enrollment-period-faq-10-28-2013.pdf.<br>HHS followed that action with additional announcements aimed at individuals seeking to enroll for coverage beginning January 1, 2014. First, on November 22, 2013, HHS extended the December 15 deadline to sign up for health coverage beginning January 1 by eight days, to December 23. Second, citing delays due to heavy use of Healthcare.gov, HHS on December 23 announced a 24-hour grace period for individuals trying to sign up for coverage beginning January 1, effectively extending the deadline to December 24. Third, HHS announced on December 24 that individuals might qualify for a special enrollment period, pursuant to ACA Section 1311(c)(6)(C), as implemented by 45 C.F.R. 155.420, if they could show that they missed the deadline for coverage beginning January 1 because of problems with Healthcare.gov. For more information, see http://www.nytimes.com/interactive/2013/12/20/us/politics/changes- and-delays-to-health-law.html?_r=1&. | ACA Section 1501(b) requires most U.S. citizens and legal residents to maintain minimum essential health coverage beginning in 2014. Individuals without coverage for three consecutive months will have to pay a penalty unless they qualify for one of the statutory exemptions.<br>CMS specified in regulation (45 C.F.R. 155.410) that the initial open enrollment period for individuals to enroll in coverage through an exchange would extend from October 1, 2013, through March 31, 2014. For individuals who sign up for coverage between the 1st and 15th of a given month, the coverage effective date is the first day of the immediately following month. However, for those who sign up between the 16th and end of a given month, the coverage effective date is the first day of the second following month. Thus, an individual who signed up on February 16, 2014, would not be insured until April 1, 2014. That individual would be uninsured for the first three months of 2014 and would have to pay a fine, unless otherwise exempt. CMS exercised its authority under IRC Section 5000A(e)(5), as added by ACA Section 1501(b), to establish a hardship exemption in order to provide relief for such individuals who waited until after February 15, 2014, to enroll. |
| 2014 Open Enrollment: Special Enrollment Periods in the Federally Facilitated Exchanges | |
| On March 26, 2014, five days before the close of the 2014 open enrollment period, CMS announced that people who attest that they have been unable to enroll in a QHP | The circumstances that warrant a special enrollment period include a natural disaster, a serious medical condition, unresolved casework, errors related to immigration |

| Summary of Administrative Action | Explanatory Notes and Comments |
|---|---|
| through the federally facilitated exchange for various specified circumstances will be eligible for a special enrollment period, pursuant to ACA Section 1311(c)(6)(C), as implemented by 45 C.F.R. 155.420. Such individuals will be able to enroll after open enrollment closes on March 31. | status, and technical problems with Healthcare.gov. For a complete list, see http://www.cms.gov/CCIIO/Resources/Regulations-and-Guidance/Downloads/complexcases-SEP-3-26-2014.pdf |
| *2014 Open Enrollment: Exceptional Circumstances in State-Based Exchanges and Retroactive Payment of Subsidies* | |
| On February 27, 2014, CMS issued guidance allowing state-based exchanges to provide advance payments of the premium tax credit and cost-sharing reductions on a retroactive basis for eligible individuals who were unable to enroll in a QHP through the exchange because IT problems prevented timely eligibility determinations. CMS considers this situation an exceptional circumstance under 45 C.F.R. 155.420.<br>Once a successful eligibility determination is obtained and the individual enrolls in the QHP through the exchange, the exchange may deem the coverage to have started on the date the individual originally submitted an application and encountered the IT problems. This would allow the individual to get the premium tax credit and costsharing reductions retroactively if they qualify based on income.<br>Additionally, if an individual covered under this exceptional circumstance has enrolled in the QHP outside of the exchange, then once that individual receives an eligibility determination for exchange coverage, the exchange may deem the individual to have been enrolled in the QHP through the exchange retroactive to the date the individual enrolled outside of the exchange. Again, this would allow the individual to get the premium tax credit and cost-sharing reductions retroactively if he or she qualifies based on income. Upon making an eligibility determination, the exchange also | Individuals must receive an eligibility determination in order to enroll in a QHP offered through an exchange and receive the premium tax credit and cost-sharing reductions authorized by the ACA.<br>The February 27, 2014, guidance is at http://www.cms.gov/CCIIO/Resources/Regulations-and-Guidance/Downloads/retroactive-advance-payments-ptc-csrs-02-27-14.pdf.<br>CMS issued clarifications to the February 27 guidance on March 14; see http://www.cms.gov/CCIIO/Resources/Fact-Sheets-and-FAQs/Downloads/retroactiveadvance-payments-ptc-csrs-03-14-14.pdf. |

**Table 1. (Continued)**

| Summary of Administrative Action | Explanatory Notes and Comments |
|---|---|
| must provide a special enrollment period under 45 C.F.R. 155.420 to allow these individuals the opportunity to change QHPs prospectively. | |
| *Renewal of Cancelled Health Plans*<br>On November 14, 2013, the Administration established a transition policy—which it encouraged state health commissioners to adopt—in response to the decision of insurers to send cancellation notices to individuals and small businesses with health plans in the individual and small group markets that do not meet the ACA's new standards for health insurance coverage. Under the policy, insurers could choose to renew such noncompliant health plans for a policy year starting between January 1, 2014, and October 1, 2014, if permitted by state insurance regulators. CMS also indicated that it would consider the impact of this transition policy in assessing whether to extend it. The intent of the policy was to allow Americans whose insurance companies cancelled their insurance coverage for 2014 to remain in their plans. See http://www.whitehouse.gov/the-press-office/2013/11/14/fact-sheet-newadministration-proposal-help-consumers-facing-cancellatio.<br>On December 19, 2013, CMS issued further clarification of the options available to consumers with cancelled policies. These consumers are eligible for a hardship exemption from the individual mandate penalty if other available options are unaffordable, or they can purchase a catastrophic plan if one is offered in their area.<br>See http://www.cms.gov/CCIIO/ Resources/Regulations-and-Guidance/Downloads/cancellation- | Under the ACA, health plans that consumers had at the time the law was enacted in 2010 were "grandfathered" in and have existed largely unchanged since the law's enactment. Grandfathered plans do not have to adopt many of the ACA's new requirements for health insurance, including coverage of essential health benefits and other consumer protections that took effect at the beginning of 2014. However, new (i.e., non-grandfathered) plans purchased since the law's enactment have to meet all the ACA requirements. For a January 8, 2014, update on state decisions regarding the transition policy on health plan cancellations, see http://www.commonwealthfund.org/ Blog/2013/Nov/State-Decisions-on-Policy-Cancellations-Fix.aspx. |

| Summary of Administrative Action | Explanatory Notes and Comments |
|---|---|
| consumer-options-12-19-2013.pdf. On March 5, 2014, CMS extended the transition policy for two years, to policy years beginning on or before October 1, 2016. Thus, at the option of state regulators, insurers who issued (or plan to issue) a policy in the individual or small group market under the November 14, 2013 transition policy may renew such policies at any time through October 1, 2016. CMS also indicated that it would consider the impact of the two-year extension in assessing whether an additional one-year extension is appropriate. CMS also extended the hardship exemption established for consumers with cancelled policies until October 1, 2016. See http://www.cms.gov/CCIIO/Resources/Regulations-and-Guidance/Downloads/transition-to-compliant-policies-03-06-2015.pdf | |
| *Exchange Applicant Eligibility and Verification* HHS's July 15, 2013, final rule on health insurance exchange eligibility and enrollment included two one-year delays regarding verification of applicant information. First, the rule permits state-based exchanges during 2014 to audit less than 100% of exchange applicants who report income at least 10% below the amount indicated by IRS and SSA records, provided the sample size used is statistically significant. The government initially had proposed an audit of all such individuals. Second, state-based exchanges will not be required until 2015 to verify applicants' information about employer coverage in order to determine eligibility for premium tax credits. During 2014 the exchanges may accept an applicant's attestation regarding employer coverage without further | Under IRC Section 36B(b), as added by ACA Section 1401(a), individuals and families who enroll in qualified health plans (QHPs) offered through an exchange are eligible for refundable premium tax credits if their income is between 100% and 400% of the federal poverty level. Under IRC Section 36B(c)(2)(C), as added by ACA Section 1401(a), individuals whose employer offers a health plan that is affordable (i.e., the employee's share of the premium does not exceed 9.5% of the employee's household income) and provides minimum value (i.e., the plan's share of the total allowed costs of benefits provided under the plan is at least 60%) are not eligible for a premium tax credit through the exchange. |

**Table 1. (Continued)**

| Summary of Administrative Action | Explanatory Notes and Comments |
|---|---|
| verification. See 78 *Federal Register* 42159, http://www.gpo.gov/fdsys/pkg/FR-2013-07-15/pdf/2013-16271.pdf. | |
| *2015 Open Enrollment*<br>On November 22, 2013, HHS announced that it was planning to delay by one month the open enrollment period for plan years that begin in 2015. The dates for the 2015 open enrollment period were included in the final rule for benefit and payment parameters for 2015, which was published on March 11, 2014. See 79 *Federal Register* 13743, http://www.gpo.gov/fdsys/pkg/FR-2014-03-11/pdf/2014-05052.pdf. | The open enrollment period for 2015 will begin November 15, 2014—instead of October 15, 2014—and extend through February 15, 2015. |
| *Employer Mandate and Insurer Reporting*<br>On July 9, 2013, the IRS provided transition relief to employers by delaying until 2015 the ACA requirement that employers with at least 50 full-time equivalent employees provide health coverage for their full-time workers or risk paying a penalty. The IRS also delayed until 2015 the requirement for employers and insurers to report certain information to the IRS. The agency indicated that these actions were taken pursuant to its administrative authority under IRC Section 7805(a) to grant transition relief when implementing new legislation. See http://www.irs.gov/pub/irs-drop/n-13-45.PDF.<br>The IRS's February 12, 2014, final rule on the ACA's employer mandate included an additional year of transition relief for employers with at least 50 but fewer than 100 full-time equivalent employees, provided the employers meet certain other requirements such as not reducing their workforce to qualify for the additional relief and maintaining previously offered coverage. These employers would not be | Generally, under IRC Section 4980H ("Shared Responsibility for Employers Regarding Health Coverage"), as added by ACA Section 1513, employers with at least 50 fulltime equivalent employees are liable for a penalty if (1) they do not offer health coverage to at least 95% of their full-time employees (and their dependents) and at least one full-time employee receives a premium tax credit for coverage purchased through an exchange; or (2) they offer health coverage to all or least 95% of full-time employees, but at least one full-time employee receives a premium tax credit for coverage purchased through an exchange because the employer didn't offer coverage to that employee or because the coverage offered was either unaffordable or did not provide minimum value (see explanatory note for "Exchange Applicant Eligibility and Verification"). IRC Section 6055, as added by ACA Section 1502(a), requires reporting by insurers, self-insuring employers, and other parties that provide health coverage.<br>IRC Section 6056, as added by ACA Section 1514(a), requires certain employers to report on the health coverage they offer to their full- |

| Summary of Administrative Action | Explanatory Notes and Comments |
|---|---|
| subject to the ACA's employer mandate until 2016. In addition, employers subject to the mandate in 2015 (i.e., those with 100 or more full-time equivalent employees) can avoid a penalty by offering coverage to 70% of their full-time employees, as opposed to 95% of such employees (as described in the explanatory notes). See 79 *Federal Register* 8543, http://www.gpo.gov/fdsys/pkg/FR-2014-02-12/pdf/2014-03082.pdf. | time employees. For more information on the ACA employer mandate, including transition relief, see http://www.irs.gov/uac/Newsroom/Questions-and-Answers-on-Employer-Shared-Responsibility-Provisions-Under-the-Affordable-Care-Act. |
| *W-2 Reporting of Employer-Sponsored Health Coverage*<br>In a series of notices, the IRS has provided transition relief to employers by giving them additional time to make any necessary changes to payroll systems and procedures in order to comply with the ACA's W-2 reporting requirement. First, it made reporting on the 2011 W-2—typically provided to employees in January 2012—optional. Second, while employers are generally required to report the cost of health benefits on the W-2 for 2012 and subsequent years, the IRS has provided transition relief for certain employers and with respect to certain types of coverage. Employers covered by the transition relief are not required to report until future guidance is issued. | IRC Section 6051(a), as amended by ACA Section 9002, generally requires the cost of employer-sponsored health coverage to be reported on Form W-2 (Wage and Tax Statement). This reporting requirement applies to taxable years beginning after December 31, 2010. For more information on the W-2 reporting requirement and associated transition relief, see http://www.irs.gov/uac/Employer-Provided-Health-Coverage-Informational-Reporting-Requirements:-Questions-and-Answers. |
| *Annual Limits on Cost-Sharing and Deductibles*<br>Plans may use more than one service provider to help administer benefits (e.g., a separate pharmacy benefits manager for coverage of pharmaceuticals), each of which may impose different cost-sharing. To allow service providers more time to coordinate their cost-sharing requirements so that the plan meets the ACA's annual cost-sharing limits, the Administration on February 20, 2013, announced a one-year grace period to allow each service provider to apply the cost-sharing limits to the | PHSA Section 2707(b), as added by ACA Section 1201, requires group health plans to ensure that any annual cost-sharing (e.g., deductibles, coinsurance, copayments) imposed under the plan for a plan year beginning on or after January 1, 2014, does not exceed the limitations established under ACA Section 1302(c)(1) and (c)(2). Under ACA Section 1302(c)(1), annual cost-sharing for a plan year beginning in 2014 may not exceed the current-law Health Savings Accounts limits; for each plan year there after these limits are indexed to the percentage increase in average per-capita premiums. |

**Table 1. (Continued)**

| Summary of Administrative Action | Explanatory Notes and Comments |
|---|---|
| benefits they administer. Under this policy, for example, many group health plans will be able to maintain separate cost-sharing limits for medical coverage (e.g., hospital and doctors' services) and for prescription drug coverage. However, this policy applies only to the first plan year beginning in 2014. See http://www.dol.gov/ebsa/faqs/ faqaca12.html. | Under ACA Section 1302(c)(2), which applies only to the small group market, the deductible for a plan year beginning in 2014 may not exceed $2,000 for individuals and $4,000 for families; again, for each plan year thereafter these limits are indexed to the percentage increase in average per-capita premiums. |
| *Pre-Existing Condition Insurance Plan (PCIP)*<br>On March 14, 2014, HHS announced that individuals enrolled in a PCIP who had not yet found new health insurance coverage through an exchange could purchase an additional month of PCIP coverage through April 30, 2014. This is the third time that HHS has extended PCIP coverage. The PCIP program was originally scheduled to terminate on January 1, 2014. However, on December 12, 2013, HHS announced that the PCIP program would be extended through the end of January 2014. Then on January 14, 2014, HHS announced that individuals could keep their PCIP coverage for two additional months, through March 31, 2014. Under the most recent announcement, PCIP participants must enroll in a new plan by April 15 for coverage to begin on May 1, if they want to avoid a lapse in coverage. | ACA Section 1101 instructed the HHS Secretary to establish a temporary program—PCIP—to provide health insurance coverage for eligible individuals who have been uninsured for six months and have a pre-existing condition. PCIP is federally administered in 23 states and DC; the remaining states administer their own PCIPs. The ACA appropriated $5 billion, to remain available without fiscal year limitation, to pay claims against (and administrative costs of) PCIPs that are in excess of premiums collected from enrollees. The federally-run PCIP and state-run PCIPs stopped accepting new enrollees on February 16, 2013, and March 2, 2013, respectively, because of the finite amount of available funding. Under the law, PCIP coverage was to end on January 1, 2014, and the Secretary was instructed to develop procedures for transitioning individuals enrolled in PCIP into qualified health plans offered through the exchanges. However, ACA Section 1101(g)(3) gave the Secretary the authority to extend PCIP coverage, if necessary, to avoid a lapse in coverage for such individuals.<br>For more information, see https://www.pcip.gov/. |
| *Basic Health Plan Option*<br>On February 7, 2013, HHS announced that implementation of the Basic Health Program (BHP) would be delayed by one | ACA Section 1331, as amended, permits states to establish a BHP in which states contract with private-sector and cooperative health plans to provide health insurance coverage for |

| Summary of Administrative Action | Explanatory Notes and Comments |
|---|---|
| year until 2015. The BHP gives states the option of using ACA subsidies to help cover certain low-income individuals whose income is too igh to qualify for Medicaid. See http://www.medicaid.gov/State-Resource-Center/FAQ-Medicaid-an-CHIP-Affordable-Care-Act-Implementation/ Downloads/FAQs-by-Topic-BHP.pdf. | certain low-income individuals not eligible for the state's Medicaid program with incomes between 133% and 200% of the federal poverty level. States that decide to offer a BHP receive federal funding equal to 95% of the value of the premium tax credits and cost-sharing subsidies that eligible individuals would have received had they purchased coverage through an exchange. For more information, see http://medicaid.gov/Basic-Health-Program/Behavioral-Health-Program.html. |
| *Small Business Health Options Program (SHOP) Exchanges*<br>HHS's June 4, 2013, final rule for the SHOP exchanges included a transition policy that delays until 2015 a requirement that SHOP exchanges provide qualified employers the option to offer employees a choice of QHPs. For plan years beginning in 2014, federally facilitated SHOP exchanges will only allow employers to select one QHP to offer to their employees, while state-based SHOP exchanges may allow employers to choose one or more QHPs to offer to their employees. See 78 *Federal Register* 33233, http://www.gpo.gov/fdsys/pkg/FR-2013-06-04/pdf/2013-13149.pdf. On November 27, 2013, HHS announced that federally facilitated SHOP exchanges will not accept online enrollments for one year, until November 2014. In the meantime, small businesses can enroll in plans listed on these exchanges through an insurance agent or broker, or directly with the insurance carrier. Note: This announcement represented the third delay in launching the online SHOP exchange, which was originally expected to be fully functional at the beginning of October 2013.<br>See http://www.hhs.gov/healthcare/ facts/blog/2013/11/direct-new-path-to- | ACA Section 1311 requires each state (or the federal government on its behalf) to establish a SHOP exchange through which small employers will be able to purchase plans for their employees. Initially, states can choose to open SHOP exchanges to companies with up to 100 employees or limit participation to companies with 50 or fewer employees. By 2016, states must open the exchanges to companies with up to 100 employees. Beginning in 2017, states have the option to open SHOP exchanges to companies with more than 100 employees. Employers with fewer than 25 employees may qualify for tax credits if they purchase insurance coverage for their employees through a SHOP exchange. For more information, see https://www.healthcare.gov/small-businesses/. |

**Table 1. (Continued)**

| Summary of Administrative Action | Explanatory Notes and Comments |
|---|---|
| shopmarketplace.html. On March 14, 2014, CMS announced that it will consider requests from states that are not yet able to enroll small businesses through their SHOP exchanges online to use the same direct enrollment approach that the federally facilitated SHOP exchanges have implemented for 2014. See http://www.cms.gov/CCIIO/ Resources/Fact-Sheetsand-FAQs/Downloads/retroactive-advance-payments-ptc-csrs-03-14-14.pdf. | |
| *Electronic Reporting* HHS's July 15, 2013, final rule on health insurance exchange eligibility and enrollment delayed until 2015 a requirement that state Medicaid agencies provide notices electronically to beneficiaries. Between October 1, 2013, and January 1, 2015, state Medicaid agencies must give individuals the choice to receive notices in electronic format or by regular mail. Agencies must ensure that an individual's choice to receive electronic notices is confirmed by regular mail, and must inform the individual of his or her right to switch to receiving notice through regular mail. [42 C.F.R. 435.918] See 78 *Federal Register* 42159, http://www.gpo.gov/fdsys/pkg/FR-2013-07-15/pdf/2013-16271.pdf. | Exchanges must also provide required notices by regular mail or, if an individual elects, electronically, provided that the specifications for electronic notices in 42 C.F.R. 435.918 are met. However, exchanges may choose to delay until 2015 the requirement in 42 C.F.R. 435.918(b)(1) that individuals who elect to receive electronic notices receive confirmation by mail. [45 C.F.R. 155.230(d)] |

Source: Prepared by the Congressional Research Service based on a review of the documents cited in the table.

## End Notes

1 The ACA was signed into law on March 23, 2010 (P.L. 111-148). On March 30, 2010, the President signed the Health Care and Education Reconciliation Act (HCERA; P.L. 111-152), which amended numerous provisions in the ACA. HCERA also included multiple new freestanding provisions related to the ACA. Several other bills enacted during the

111th and 112th Congresses made additional changes to selected ACA provisions. All references to the ACA in this report refer, collectively, to the law as amended and to the related HCERA provisions.

[2] A detailed examination of the ACA is beyond the scope of this report. Readers who are unfamiliar with the ACA's provisions to restructure the private health insurance market and expand access to affordable health insurance through the competitive marketplaces—or exchanges—and the expansion of state Medicaid programs will find numerous CRS products that provide more in-depth information on the law at http://www.crs.gov/pages/subissue.aspx?cliid=3746& parentid=13&preview=False.

[3] Internal Revenue Service, "Transition Relief for 2014 Under §§ 6055 (Information Reporting), 6056 (Information Reporting) and 4980H (Employer Shared Responsibility Provisions)," Notice 2013-45, July 9, 2013, http://www.irs.gov/pub/irs-drop/n-13-45.PDF.

[4] The White House, "Fact Sheet: New Administration Proposal to Help Consumers Facing Cancellations," November 14, 2013, http://www.whitehouse.gov/the-press-office/2013/11/14/fact-sheet-new-administration-proposal-helpconsumers-facing-cancellatio.

[5] Department of Health & Human Services, Centers for Medicare & Medicaid Services, "Insurance Standards Bulletin Series - Extension of Transitional Policy through October 1, 2016," March 5, 2014, http://www.cms.gov/CCIIO/ Resources/Regulations-and-Guidance/Downloads/transition-to-compliant-policies-03-06-2015.pdf.

[6] Department of Health & Human Services, Centers for Medicare & Medicaid Services, "Guidance for Issuers on Special Enrollment Periods for Complex Cases in the Federally-facilitated Marketplace after the Initial Open Enrollment Period," March 26, 2014, http://www.cms.gov/CCIIO/Resources/Regulations-and-Guidance/Downloads/ complex-cases-SEP-3-26-2014.pdf.

[7] Simon Lazarus, "Delaying Parts of Obamacare: 'Blatantly Illegal' or Routine Adjustment?," The Atlantic, July 17, 2013, http://www.theatlantic.com/national/archive/2013/07/delaying-parts-of-obamacare-blatantly-illegal-or-routineadjustment/277873/.

[8] Timothy Stoltzfus Jost and Simon Lazarus, "Obama's ACA Delays - Breaking the Law or Making it Work?," New England Journal of Medicine, April 2, 2014, http://www.nejm.org/doi/pdf/10.1056/NEJMp1403294.

[9] Section 7805(a) of the Internal Revenue Code; 26 U.S.C. § 7805(a).

[10] Letter from Mark J. Mazur, Assistant Secretary for Tax Policy, to Honorable Fred Upton, Chairman, Committee on Energy and Commerce, July 9, 2013, http://democrats .energycommerce.house.gov/sites/default/files/documents/UptonTreasury-ACA-2013-7-9.pdf. For a legal analysis of the Administration's decision to delay enforcement of the employer mandate, see CRS Legal Sidebar, Obama Administration Delays Implementation of ACA's Employer Responsibility Requirements: A Brief Legal Overview, posted July 8, 2013, http://www.crs.gov/LegalSidebar/ details.aspx?ProdId=582.

[11] Nichclas Bagley, "The Legality of Delaying Key Elements of the ACA," New England Journal of Medicine, April 2, 2014, http://www.nejm.org/doi/pdf/10.1056/NEJMp1402641. For a legal analysis of the Administration's decision to permit insurers to renew noncompliant policies for individuals and small businesses, see CRS Legal Sidebar, Obama Administration's "Fix" for Insurance Cancellations: A Legal Overview, posted November 18, 2013, http://www.crs.gov/LegalSidebar/details.aspx?ProdId=724.

[12] CRS Report R43289, Legislative Actions to Repeal, Defund, or Delay the Affordable Care Act, by C. Stephen Redhead and Janet Kinzer.

In: The Affordable Care Act
Editor: Eileen H. Blume

ISBN: 978-1-63117-871-9


*Chapter 4*

# FREE EXERCISE OF RELIGION BY SECULAR ORGANIZATIONS AND THEIR OWNERS: IMPLICATIONS FOR THE AFFORDABLE CARE ACT (ACA)*

*Cynthia Brougher*

## SUMMARY

The Supreme Court's grant of review in *Conestoga Wood Specialties Corp. v. Secretary of U.S. Department of Health and Human Services* and *Hobby Lobby Stores v. Sebelius*, along with recent federal court decisions, has highlighted the ongoing controversy over the scope of the Affordable Care Act's (ACA's) contraceptive coverage requirement, which requires an employer to provide certain contraceptive coverage to its employees under its group health plan. Some employers have objected to the requirement, citing objections to the facilitation of the use of contraceptives in conflict with the religious tenets by which their businesses operate. An analogous issue has arisen in state courts in the context of same-sex weddings. Several private businesses that qualify as public accommodations have objected to state requirements that they provide services without discriminating based on sexual orientation despite the owners' religious objections to same-sex marriage. These

* This is an edited, reformatted and augmented version of a Congressional Research Service publication, No. R43329, dated March 21, 2014.

issues have raised a novel legal question for the courts: What rights do secular businesses that operate for profit have to pursue legal claims to protect their religious exercise?

Although a number of statutory exemptions exist to protect individuals and organizations' religious beliefs and objections (e.g., employment discrimination under Title VII, disability discrimination under the Americans with Disabilities Act, etc.), courts have applied those exemptions only to individuals and nonprofit, religious organizations. A number of legal challenges to the contraceptive coverage requirement have examined a range of questions related to the rights of these businesses. As a threshold question, courts have had to analyze whether the business itself is eligible for protection under the Religious Freedom Restoration Act (RFRA) and Free Exercise jurisprudence. The businesses have asserted that they qualify as "persons" under RFRA and, in the alternative, that they are entitled to pursue their claims on behalf of their owners under what is known as the "pass-through" theory of corporate rights. Courts have also considered whether the business owners may pursue independent legal claims asserting their objections, or if their individual rights are forfeited at the time of the company's incorporation.

If a court determines that the business or its owners are eligible for free exercise protection, it may then consider the merits of the case, including whether the mandate constitutes a substantial burden on religious exercise; whether the government has a compelling interest to do so; and whether the government used the least restrictive means to achieve that interest. Five federal circuit courts have considered these questions in the context of the contraceptive coverage requirement, and have reached different conclusions on the range of questions raised.

This report examines the constitutional and statutory protections related to free exercise of religion, including current Supreme Court interpretations, as well as judicial and legislative avoidance of defining the parameters of religious belief. It also discusses significant examples of existing religious exemptions in current law, including employment nondiscrimination, health care, and public accommodations law. Finally, it analyzes recent federal judicial decisions that have considered the religious freedom rights of commercial entities whose owners have religious objections to the contraceptive coverage requirement.

Recent court decisions have highlighted the ongoing controversy over the scope of the Affordable Care Act's (ACA's) contraceptive coverage requirement[1] and, more generally, whether religious freedom rights extend to commercial entities as well as nonprofits and individuals.[2] Although illustrated by the contraceptive coverage requirement, the question of whether secular, for-profit entities qualify for religious freedom protections reaches farther than the ongoing debate over ACA. Congress has enacted a number of exemptions to accommodate religious objections to legislative requirements, but those exemptions generally have been limited to individuals and nonprofit organizations.[3] That is, for-profit entities' right to exercise religion generally has not been recognized in existing law. Litigation of the contraceptive coverage requirement as well as cases involving commercial entities' objections to providing services for same-sex wedding ceremonies reflects heightened attention in courts to the question of accommodation for such objections.[4] Several federal courts and some state decisions that have considered the issue have reached different conclusions, and the U.S. Supreme Court, by granting certiorari in *Conestoga* and *Hobby Lobby Store*, appears poised to provide guidance on this issue in the future.[5]

This report examines the constitutional and statutory protections related to free exercise of religion, including current Supreme Court interpretations, as well as judicial and legislative avoidance of defining the parameters of religious belief. It also discusses significant examples of existing religious exemptions in current law, including employment nondiscrimination, health care, and public accommodations law. Finally, it analyzes recent federal judicial decisions that have considered the religious freedom rights of commercial entities whose owners have religious objections to the contraceptive coverage requirement.

## LEGAL PROTECTIONS PREVENTING GOVERNMENT INTERFERENCE WITH RELIGIOUS BELIEF

Since 1879, the Supreme Court has drawn an important distinction in religious freedom cases, noting that religious exercise includes both protection of religious beliefs and actions based on those beliefs.[6] The Court has permitted the government to regulate actions stemming from religious belief, but not the religious belief itself.[7] Over time, the constitutional protection against interference with religious beliefs has been augmented by statute.[8]

## Constitutional Protection

The First Amendment states that "Congress shall make no law respecting an establishment of religion, or prohibiting the free exercise thereof.... "[9] Historically, the U.S. Supreme Court had interpreted the Free Exercise Clause to require that the government show a compelling interest for any government action that interfered with a person's exercise of religious beliefs.[10] However, in 1990, the Court reinterpreted that standard, issuing a decision in *Employment Division, Department of Human Resources of Oregon v. Smith* in which the Court explained that the Free Exercise Clause never "relieve[s] an individual of the obligation to comply with a valid and neutral law of general applicability."[11] The Court's decision lowered the constitutional baseline of protection, meaning that laws that do not specifically target religion are not subject to heightened review under the First Amendment. Accordingly, it is less likely that individuals and entities with religious objections will be able to argue successfully for constitutional protection from laws that only incidentally burden their religious exercise.

The Court's decision in *Smith* emphasized that the legislature remained free to consider whether an exemption for the accommodation of religious exercise would be appropriate through the political process, even if the exemption were not required as a matter of constitutional law.[12] In other words, religious exemptions generally are a matter of legislative discretion under current Court jurisprudence.

## Statutory Protection

Congress responded to *Smith* by enacting the Religious Freedom Restoration Act (RFRA), which essentially reinstated the heightened standard of protection applied to government actions that interfered with the free exercise of religion.[13] RFRA requires that a statute or regulation of general applicability may substantially burden a person's exercise of religion only if it (1) furthers a compelling governmental interest and (2) uses the least restrictive means to further that interest.[14] RFRA has been interpreted to apply only to federal government actions, but it should be noted that state legislatures have enacted similar protection against interference with religious exercise by state government actions.[15] Legal protection under RFRA is a matter of statutory law, meaning that a future Congress may choose to preempt RFRA or otherwise amend the protection it provides.[16]

## Avoidance of Defining the Scope of Religious Belief

One of the principles underlying the First Amendment is the prevention of government interference with religious institutions and matters of religion. The Court has long recognized that such institutions have a right to address their internal matters independently and without interference from government institutions.[17] Furthermore, such action by the government likely would entangle the legal system in an inquiry of religious doctrine, suggesting the type of probing interference historically considered unconstitutional by the Court.[18] The Court has explained that the First Amendment ensures the freedom to believe, even if those beliefs cannot be proven, and thus has prohibited courts from judging the veracity of religious beliefs.[19] Accordingly, Congress and the Court have refused to define with specificity what constitutes religion.

While courts must avoid determining the validity of religious beliefs, at times it may be necessary to determine whether beliefs would qualify as religious for certain purposes, including religious exemptions for statutory requirements. To do so, the Supreme Court has explained that the test for whether a belief is religious depends on whether the belief is sincerely held and whether it is applied consistently by the objector.[20] This test illustrates a subjective standard by which courts evaluate the religious practice of parties challenging interference with religious exercise.

Legislative attempts to define religion have reflected similar aversion to stating explicitly the parameters of religious belief, practice, or exercise. Statutory definitions related to religion often use the word to define itself. For example, Title VII of the Civil Rights Act of 1964 includes an exemption for religious institutions and is often used as a model for exemptions in other contexts.[21] Title VII defines religion to include "all aspects of religious observance and practice, as well as belief.... "[22] Religious practices and observances are defined "to include moral or ethical beliefs as to what is right and wrong which are sincerely held with the strength of traditional religious views."[23]

The aversion of courts and legislatures to identify specific parameters of religion often leads to the adoption of general exemptions. If an exemption is specifically tailored to identify particular religions that would qualify, it may violate the Establishment Clause by indicating a preference of particular sects or exclusion of others.[24] However, if the exemption is offered generally to individuals or entities having a religious belief in conflict with the requirement interfering with religious practice, it likely will meet the subjective standard used by the court and avoid both the appearance of preferential treatment in violation of the Establishment Clause as well as the infringement on religious exercise in violation of the Free Exercise Clause.

# Selected Examples of Religious Objections and Related Exemptions Affecting Secular Organizations

The statutory exemptions discussed below attempt to accommodate religious objections to legislative mandates. These exemptions are limited to the statutory context in which they were adopted and, therefore, the definitions enacted in statute or adopted by courts cannot be conferred to other contexts automatically, unless the exemption was written in such a way that cross-references one exemption to incorporate it into another. These exemptions and their interpretations serve as examples of how Congress and the courts have addressed the scope of religious objections thus far.

## Employment Non-Discrimination and Conflicts Between Religious Beliefs in the Workplace

Title VII of the Civil Rights Act of 1964 prohibits discrimination in employment on the basis of race, color, religion, sex, or national origin.[25] It prohibits employers from discriminating against employees on the basis of their religious beliefs and requires employers to make reasonable accommodations for employees' religious practices.[26] However, Congress has recognized that while these provisions protect employees' religious exercise, restrictions on employment decisions by religious employers may interfere with the employer's religious practices.

As a result, Title VII includes exemptions for religious entities, allowing qualifying employers to consider religion in hiring decisions. The general exemption available to religious organizations states that the prohibition against religious discrimination does not apply to "a religious corporation, association, educational institution, or society with respect to the employment of individuals of a particular religion to perform work connected with the carrying on by such corporation, association, educational institution, or society of its activities."[27] Title VII also includes a separate, but similar exemption that applies specifically to religious educational institutions. That exemption allows educational institutions "to hire and employ employees of a particular religion if [the institution] is, in whole or in substantial part, owned, supported, controlled, or managed by a particular religion or by a particular [religious organization], or if the curriculum of [the institution] is directed toward the propagation of a particular religion."[28]

Title VII's religious exemption often is used as a model for other religious exemptions, but it does not define which organizations would qualify for exemption. The Supreme Court has declined to review cases in which the parameters of the exception are unclear, and courts have not established a uniform standard, though many have considered the issue. For example, the U.S. Court of Appeals for the Ninth Circuit explained that an entity would qualify for exemption "if it is organized for a religious purpose, is engaged primarily in carrying out that purpose, holds itself out to the public as an entity for carrying out that purpose, and does not engage primarily or substantially in the exchange of goods or services for money beyond nominal amounts."[29] Overall, lower courts generally have appeared to agree upon several factors relevant to deciding whether an organization qualifies for exemption, including (1) the purpose or mission of the organization; (2) the ownership, affiliation, or source of financial support of the organization; (3) requirements placed upon staff and members of the organization; and (4) the extent of religious practices in or the religious nature of the products and services offered by the organization and whether it operates for a profit.[30]

## Conflicts Arising from Religious Practices Related to Health Benefits Available in Group Health Plans

As discussed earlier in this report, the contraceptive coverage requirement enacted under ACA has brought the debate over which organizations qualify as "religious" in order to claim legal protection from generally applicable policy mandates. The contraceptive coverage requirement requires that group health plans and health insurance issuers provide coverage for certain preventive health services, including a range of contraceptives, without imposing cost-sharing requirements.[31] Among the stated goals and benefits of the preventive health services requirements at issue are the improvement of public health and the equitable distribution of costs for preventive services, both of which have been deemed compelling interests by courts when considering claims of interference with religious exercise.[32] However, some employers have objected to the requirement for contraceptive coverage, arguing that doing so would mean facilitating access to services that directly conflict with their religious beliefs regarding human reproduction.

Accordingly, implementing regulations have been adopted that create an exemption from compliance for certain religious employers and an accommodation for other entities with objections to the required coverage.[33] Employers who do not qualify for exemption or accommodation must include contraceptive coverage as part of group health plans offered to their employees. Generally, "religious employers" are exempt from the requirement, meaning their employees are not provided coverage for contraceptives through the employer or the issuer.[34] The regulations define a religious employer as "an organization that is organized and operates as a nonprofit entity and is referred to in section 6033(a)(3)(A)(i) or (iii) of the Internal Revenue Code of 1986, as amended."[35] The referenced subsections of the tax code respectively refer to "churches, their integrated auxiliaries, and conventions or associations of churches" and to "the exclusively religious activities of any religious order."[36]

Additionally, other eligible employers with objections to the coverage of contraceptive service may qualify for an accommodation, meaning that their employees must be offered contraceptive coverage but the cost is covered by the health plan issuer, rather than the employer.[37] To qualify for the accommodation, an organization must (1) have religious objections to the provision of coverage for any of the required contraceptive services; (2) be organized and operate as a nonprofit entity; (3) hold itself out as a religious organization; and (4) self-certify that it meets these criteria.[38]

By the definitions of religious employer and eligible organizations, an entity seeking to avoid compliance with the contraceptive coverage requirement must be a nonprofit. A number of employers that do not qualify for either the exemption or accommodation have challenged the scope of the regulations, particularly the exclusion of for-profit entities that would be required to provide coverage in conflict with asserted religious objections.[39] These cases are discussed in further detail later in this report.

## Denial of Services to Same-Sex Couples by Places of Public Accommodation

Title II of the Civil Rights Act of 1964 prohibits discrimination in public accommodations.[40] Public accommodations, which are defined as establishments that serve the public and that have a connection to interstate commerce, include hotels, restaurants, and entertainment venues.[41] Federal protection against discrimination by entities qualifying as public accommodations under Title II applies only if the discrimination is based on race, color, religion, or national origin, and does not include sexual orientation.[42] However, some states have adopted broader analogous protections that prohibit public accommodations from discriminating in the provision of goods and services on the basis of sexual orientation.[43]

Certain public accommodations have objected to the lack of exemption for entities with religious objections to same-sex relationships. These objections have arisen mainly in the context of same-sex marriage and civil union ceremonies.[44]

However, there also have been examples of objections to equal treatment of same-sex families in other contexts, such as adoption services, medical services, and housing.[45] As a general rule, although states that have recognized same-sex marriage may have included a religious exemption to protect the rights of religious clergy to refuse to perform or sanctify such unions, only some states have provided similar protection for other officials or for organizations that may provide services related to weddings.[46]

Despite the possible lack of exemptions available under public accommodations laws for individuals with religious objections to certain sexual orientations, entities with such objections may avoid violating the law in many instances if they limit the availability of related services to certain purposes.

In other words, if the public accommodations law applies only to entities that are generally open or otherwise available to the public, an entity may limit its liability under the law by restricting access for a particular purpose. For example, if an entity is open to the public for weddings and other such ceremonies, but attempts to deny a same-sex couple from having access, it likely would be in violation of public accommodations law.[47] On the other hand, if the entity is open to the public for other purposes, but not for weddings, then it would not violate the public accommodations law. The controversy arises in these scenarios when an entity attempts to make a service available to most of the public, but attempts to exclude a particular group for the same purpose.

# Eligibility of Secular Entities for Exemptions Based on Religious Objections

The U.S. Supreme Court has never considered the merits of a case challenging the eligibility of secular, for-profit corporations to claim protection for religious exercise, although it has recognized the rights of individuals and of religious, nonprofit organizations to claim such protection.[48] Recent controversy arising from the contraceptive coverage mandate has brought the question of secular entities' religious freedom rights before a number of federal courts, resulting in a split among the federal circuits, and has led the Supreme Court to grant review of two of the key cases on this issue.[49]

Among the questions posed by the contraceptive cases are whether secular corporations may pursue legal challenges related to religious freedom under either the First Amendment or RFRA; whether the corporations' for-profit status should be considered in eligibility for legal protection; whether the religious rights of the owners of closely held corporations "pass-through" to the corporation itself; and whether those owners may pursue distinct legal challenges separate from the corporation. These threshold questions must precede consideration of the merits of any such corporation or owners' claim that the mandate imposes a substantial burden on religious exercise.

It is important to note that the contraceptive cases discussed below consider whether the parties seeking exemption qualify for injunctive relief to avoid compliance with the pending contraceptive coverage requirements. If injunctive relief is denied, the parties who refuse to comport with the requirement face significant financial penalties for the duration of the litigation. Decisions to grant or deny such preliminary injunctions determine, in part, whether the parties have a likelihood of success on the merits, such that forcing them to comply during the pending challenge would result in a violation of their religious exercise rights in the meantime. Courts that have determined that the corporations or owners have met the threshold requirements mentioned above, therefore, consider the merits of the decision, but their decision does not constitute a final judgment on the merits of the case.

Three of the five circuits (Seventh, Tenth, and D.C.) that have issued decisions on the contraceptive mandate have granted preliminary injunctive relief under RFRA, finding that either the corporation, its owners, or both may assert rights under the statute and that the mandate imposes a substantial burden that lacks a compelling interest achieved by the least restrictive means.[50] The remaining two circuits (Third and Sixth) have held that secular corporations do not qualify for protection under RFRA.[51] Each of the employers bringing these challenges is a closely held corporation that is family owned or controlled. The companies generally offer secular goods and services (e.g., craft supplies, cabinet manufacturing, automotive and medical manufacturing, grocery services, and construction).[52] Courts and the owners of these companies generally have conceded that they are not religious organizations, but instead are commercial entities that are operated in accordance with the owners' religious principles.

## Historic Exclusion from Eligibility for Exemption under Title VII

Early consideration of whether secular corporations could qualify for legal protection of religious exercise arose in the context of Title VII, which requires that parties seeking exemption be religious organizations. That litigation treated the rights of a for-profit corporation and its owners as synonymous, but illustrated a reluctance to apply Title VII's religious exemption to for-profit, secular organizations. In *Equal Employment Opportunity Commission v. Townley Engineering & Manufacturing Co.*, the U.S. Court of Appeals for the Ninth Circuit held that a closely held corporation that manufactured mining equipment founded by owners with the intent to operate their business in accordance with their Christian faith could not be considered a qualifying religious organization for the purposes of Title VII.[53] The court explained that the exemption for religious corporations was not intended to cover businesses like the manufacturing company in the case.

In its decision, the court emphasized that corporations would qualify for protection under the statute's exemption only if their purpose and character were primarily religious.[54] The court found that the company's status as a for-profit organization demonstrated a secular entity.[55] Additional factors indicating its secular identity included the production of secular products, the lack of affiliation with or support from a church, and the lack of religious purpose in the company's articles of incorporation.[56] The owners' religious activities and statements, even if used in their official capacity within the business, were insufficient to overcome the secular characterization, according to the court.[57]

However, the court also recognized that the owners of that company were protected by their Free Exercise rights which Title VII could not affect.[58] As discussed further below, the court addressed the accompanying Free Exercise claim as an issue of the owners' constitutional rights, not the company's. Ultimately, it found that the owners' Free Exercise rights may be affected under Title VII, but that such limitation was justified by the overriding governmental interest.[59] According to the court, "[w]here the practices of employer and employee conflict ..., it is not inappropriate to require the employer, who structures the workplace to a substantial degree, to travel the extra mile in adjusting its free exercise rights, if any, to accommodate the employee's Title VII rights."[60] The court noted that the owners may continue to require employees to comport with their religious beliefs as adopted in the scope of the business, but that it must provide the option for employees with objections to be excused.[61] In other words, under the court's rationale, owners' decisions based on religious beliefs need not be voluntary for all employees, but must be voluntary to employees with religious objections.

The *Townley* decision illustrates the distinction between religious and secular organizations' eligibility for religious exemptions. However, it is important to keep in mind that statutory exemptions are applied within the parameters of their respective statutes. That is, if a court interprets the Title VII exemption to be limited to religious organizations only, that limitation does not transfer to religious exemptions in other statutes. Courts may review the interpretation of similar exemptions for guidance in understanding the scope of another exemption, but they are not bound to apply the same scope to all exemptions. As the Court has recognized, Congress is empowered to enact and limit the scope of statutory exemptions at its discretion.[62]

## Rights of Secular Corporations Claiming Interference with Religious Exercise

The rights of secular corporations to challenge governmental mandates that infringe upon the religious beliefs by which the businesses are operated largely depends on whether courts recognize the corporations as protected by the particular provision of law. In the context of the contraceptive coverage mandate, corporations have asserted their rights as persons protected by RFRA and Free Exercise jurisprudence generally, and they have asserted their rights as passed to them by their owners. Circuit courts have split regarding whether corporations may assert these rights under the former theory, but the circuits that have considered contraceptive mandate challenges under the so-called passed through theory have rejected it as grounds for the corporation to assert a legal challenge.

**Recognizing Privately Held Corporations as Persons under RFRA**

RFRA prohibits governmental burdens on "a person's exercise of religion" but does not define person under the statute.[63] In the absence of a definition within the statute itself, courts have looked to the Dictionary Act, which provides guidance for the meaning of common terms used in legislation. The Dictionary Act states that when "determining the meaning of any Act of Congress, unless the context indicates otherwise ... the word[] 'person' ... include[s] corporations, companies, associations, firms, partnerships, societies, and joint stock companies, as well as individuals."[64]

The Third and Sixth Circuits—the two courts that have denied contraceptive coverage challenges so far—held that the companies raising the challenge could not "exercise religion" and therefore could not avail themselves of RFRA's protection.[65] That is, even if the contraceptive mandate burdened the companies, lacked a compelling interest, or could have been implemented by other means, secular companies have no legal recourse because they are not protected under the statute. Under the Sixth Circuit's interpretation of the Dictionary Act, "RFRA's relevant context [shows] strong indications that Congress did not intend to include corporations primarily organized for secular, profit-seeking purposes as 'persons' under RFRA."[66] The court explained that the purpose of RFRA was to restore free exercise protections historically applied by the Supreme Court, "which were fundamentally personal."[67] According to the court, "Congress did not intend to expand the scope of the Free Exercise Clause" and although the Court's historic interpretation recognized free exercise rights of certain individuals engaged in for-profit businesses and nonprofit religious organizations, "it has never recognized similar rights on behalf of corporations pursuing secular ends for profit."[68]

In June 2013, the U.S. Court of Appeals for the Tenth Circuit issued a surprising decision in light of the historic exclusion of secular companies from religious exemption in other contexts, a decision with which the U.S. Court of Appeals for the Seventh Circuit agreed in November 2013. In *Hobby Lobby Stores v. Sebelius*, the Tenth Circuit held that two family-owned and operated for-profit, secular corporations could be considered "persons" whose religious exercise would be protected under RFRA.[69] Relying upon the plain text of the Dictionary Act, the courts found that the companies could be eligible for protection under RFRA.[70] The courts noted that judicial precedent, including Supreme Court jurisprudence, recognized the religious exercise rights of corporations and organizations, although the cases cited involved only religiously affiliated corporations.[71] The courts explicitly rejected the argument that religious exemptions are limited to religiously affiliated, nonprofit entities "by implication from judicial interpretation of two unrelated employment-nondiscrimination statutes."[72] Citing Title VII as an example of an exemption restricted to "religious" entities, the Seventh Circuit explained that Congress would have indicated a similar restriction had it intended to impose the same limitation on eligibility for protection under RFRA.[73] Rather, RFRA does not indicate an explicit limitation and as a result, the Seventh and Tenth Circuits held that RFRA's protection must be interpreted more broadly to allow secular organizations to seek protection for religious exercise.

It is notable that the Tenth Circuit implied that some secular businesses may be distinguished from protection under RFRA.[74] Though it recognized that closely held companies, like those in the case before it, exercised religion openly and proselytize as a form of religious exercise, the court acknowledged the difficulty of determining the sincerity of religious belief and religious exercise of a large, publicly traded corporation.[75] The *Hobby Lobby* decision was confined to the smaller, family-owned, closely held corporations, which the court explained could demonstrate adherence to a set of religious beliefs in the course of their business dealings in addition to its proselytizing activities. Courts generally avoid deciding issues beyond the scope of the cases before them, so any decision on which secular businesses may be eligible for RFRA protection is still undecided by any court. However, the Tenth Circuit's reasoning arguably may appear to be internally inconsistent. It relies on a broad reading of the term person under the Dictionary Act when determining that "persons" under RFRA could include either type of corporation—religious or secular—because the type of corporation is not explicitly restricted to religious corporations. However, it then implies that it would question whether eligible secular corporations include both closely held and publicly traded corporations, despite having stated that there is no indication of a restriction on the type of corporation that would qualify as a person.

## Potential Distinction between for-Profit and Nonprofit Entities

Courts have not seemed to focus solely on a corporation's for-profit status when determining its eligibility for free exercise protections as much as they have addressed the corporation's status as a secular or religious entity. In some discussions, these distinctions appear to be used interchangeably, i.e., if a company operates for profit, it is a secular corporation, whereas religious corporations are assumed to be nonprofit. For example, the Third and Sixth Circuits treated the characterizations jointly, both finding that the companies were simultaneously for-profit and secular.[76]

As discussed above, the Tenth Circuit held that for-profit, secular corporations could exercise religion and that the companies in that case had done so through their engagement in evangelism through religious advertising purchased by the business. The remaining circuits have explained that a corporation's commercial status is not determinative in its eligibility for free exercise protection:

> It's common ground that *nonprofit* religious corporations exercise religion in the sense that their activities are religiously motivated. So unless there is something disabling about mixing profit-seeking and religious practice, it follows that a faith-based, for-profit corporation can claim free-exercise protection to the extent that an aspect of its conduct is religiously motivated.[77]

The Seventh Circuit noted that the question of whether an entity's for-profit status would impact its ability to claim free exercise protections has never been decided by the Supreme Court, but that the Court had considered free exercise claims in other commercial contexts.[78] The Court indeed has recognized and adjudicated free exercise claims brought by individuals related to for-profit activities. In employment discrimination cases, courts have upheld free exercise rights of employees despite their claims arising from issues related to wages in commercial jobs.[79] The Seventh Circuit also referenced a free exercise case in which merchants challenged Sunday-closing laws, stating "if profit-making alone was enough to disqualify the merchants from bringing the claim, the Court surely would have said so. It did not. Instead, the Court addressed and rejected their free-exercise claim on the merits."[80] Finally, courts have pointed to the Court's decision in *United States v. Lee*, in which an Amish man sought an exemption from paying social security taxes for his employees because the program conflicted with his religious beliefs.[81] The Seventh Circuit concluded that "[t]hese cases show that far from categorically excluding profit-seekers from the scope of the free-exercise right, the Supreme Court has considered their claims on the merits, granting exemptions in some and not others based on the compelling-interest test."[82]

The Tenth Circuit agreed, noting that the Court's analysis of these cases did not depend on corporate status:

> [W]e cannot see why an individual operating for-profit retains Free Exercise protections but an individual who incorporates—even as the sole shareholder—does not, even though he engages in the exact same activities as before. This cannot be about the protections of the corporate form, such as limited liability and tax rates. Religious associations can incorporate, gain those protections, and nonetheless retain their Free Exercise rights.[83]

As discussed earlier, profit-status and commercial activity has been considered relevant in analyses of organizations' eligibility for exemption under certain statutes such as Title VII. However, it does not appear to be dispositive in cases involving eligibility for RFRA. Rather, courts' opinions seem to focus on whether the entity can practice religion, regardless of whether it profits while doing so. The critical inquiry appears to be the nature of religious exercise. As some decisions have noted, such entities cannot worship or exercise religion in the traditional sense,[84] but as others have noted, these entities can express religious values, which may also be encompassed as a form of religious exercise.[85] It may be argued that an entity's for-profit status would not affect the analysis if the business itself is providing a good or service somehow related to its religious values. However, if the religious nature of the business is merely aspirational, e.g., limited to religious principles stated in the company's mission and does not extend into business operations, it may be argued that the business is not exercising religion. The difficulty with such arguments is that courts would need to decide whether the religious beliefs and activities are sufficient to be considered religious exercise protected under the law, an inquiry generally avoided by any court as discussed earlier in this report.

## Direct Protection under the U.S. Constitution

Although it appears widely accepted that the contraceptive coverage requirement would be considered a neutral law of general applicability that does not target religious practice and therefore would not be subject to First Amendment protection, the expansion of the Supreme Court's First Amendment jurisprudence in other areas has led to questions regarding the scope of the religion clauses. In 2010, the Supreme Court issued a landmark decision in *Citizens United v. Federal Election Commission*, in which it held that "First Amendment protection extends to corporations," citing a line of cases recognizing Free Speech rights of corporations.[86] The Court noted its rejection of "the argument that political speech of corporations or other associations should be treated differently under the First Amendment simply because such associations are not 'natural persons.'"[87] *Citizens United* examined the scope of the Free Speech Clause of the First Amendment, but did not address the application of the remainder of the First Amendment (including the religious clauses) to corporations.

The Tenth Circuit's decision in *Hobby Lobby* raised questions of the scope of First Amendment protections that may be available to secular corporations seeking protection of their religious exercise. The court relied on *Citizens United* to demonstrate that corporations may express themselves as a matter of religious exercise for the purposes of RFRA, explaining that "the Free Exercise Clause is *not* a purely personal guarantee" but instead extends to associations, even if those associations have organized themselves by incorporation.[88] Noting that "religious conduct includes religious expression, which can be communicated by individuals and for-profit corporations alike," the court stated that the companies' efforts to proselytize through the purchase of newspaper advertisements that encouraged readers to "know Jesus as Lord and Savior" constituted protected religious exercise:[89]

> Because [the companies] express themselves for religious purposes, the First Amendment logic of *Citizens United*, where the Supreme Court has recognized a First Amendment right of for-profit corporations to express themselves for political purposes, applies as well. We see no reason the Supreme Court would recognize constitutional protection for a corporation's political expression but not its religious expression.[90]

The court's decision was not based on its assessment of the constitutional right, but it relied on the *Citizens United* theory to demonstrate corporations' ability to exercise religion and therefore qualify for protection under RFRA. The Seventh Circuit, which reached the same conclusion as the Tenth Circuit on the question of whether secular corporations could claim protection as persons protected by RFRA and the corporations' likelihood of success on the merits, explained that its decision centered on statutory interpretation of RFRA and avoided defining the parameters of the constitutional rights involved.[91]

However, other circuits have disagreed with the Tenth Circuit's conclusion, emphasizing that the Free Speech and Free Exercise Clauses are distinct legal protections with separate precedential history and rationales that cannot be transferred between the two. The Third Circuit rejected the idea that the clauses' grouping in the same constitutional amendment meant they "must be interpreted jointly."[92] It explained that "*Citizens United* is grounded in the notion that the Court has a long history of protecting corporations' right to free speech" but that there is no "similar history of courts providing free exercise protection to corporations."[93]

The D.C. Circuit likewise held that secular corporations could not exercise religion for purposes of RFRA or the First Amendment.[94] That court found that free exercise rights had been granted to individuals but that such rights also applied to groups, noting "the foundational principle that religious bodies—representing a communion of faith and a community of believers—are entitled to the shield of the Free Exercise Clause."[95] The court recognized that the Supreme Court had a long history of cases "recognizing that all corporations speak" but "has only indicated that people and churches worship."[96] The Court's silence with respect to secular corporations did not provide the D.C. Circuit with sufficient legal basis to support a right to free exercise by such organizations.

## Protection under the Pass-Through Theory of Corporate Rights

Companies challenging the contraceptive mandate have sought relief under the pass-through theory of corporate rights introduced in the *Townley* case, discussed earlier. In *Townley*, the Ninth Circuit framed the constitutional issue in the case as one of the owners' rights. It explained that the company was "merely an instrument through and by which [its owners] express their religious beliefs" and held that it was "unnecessary to address the abstract issue whether a for profit corporation has rights under the Free Exercise Clause independent of those of its shareholders and officers. [The company] presents no rights of its own different from or greater than its owners' rights."[97] The court provided little more discussion to explain its decision on that point, but it affirmed its holding in *Townley* in 2009, "declin[ing] to decide whether a for-profit corporation can assert its own rights under the Free Exercise Clause and instead examin[ing] the rights at issue as those of the corporate owners."[98] In that case, the court explained that the corporation was "an extension of the beliefs of the members of the [owning] family, and that the beliefs of the ... family are the beliefs of [the corporation]. Thus, [the company] does not present any free exercise rights of its own different from or greater than its owners' rights. ...[A]s in Townley, [the corporation] has standing to assert the free exercise rights of its owners."[99]

Other courts generally have rejected the Ninth Circuit's recognition of pass-through rights. The D.C. Circuit characterized the argument that a corporation which is owned by a few individuals sharing the same religious values by which they operate the company could serve as a surrogate of the owners' beliefs as "logically and structurally appealing."[100] However, the court noted that the *Townley* precedent did not provide sufficient "legal substantiation" and ultimately held that it "had no basis for concluding a secular organization can exercise religion."[101]

The Third and Sixth Circuits have rejected the pass-through theory of corporate standing as well, explaining that the nature of incorporation negates the ability of owners to assert their rights through the corporate business. The Third Circuit opined that the Ninth Circuit's rationale was based on "erroneous assumptions" about the nature of incorporation:

> It is a fundamental principle that "incorporation's basic purpose is to create a distinct legal entity, with legal rights, obligations, powers and privileges different from those of the natural individuals who created" the corporation. The "passed through" doctrine fails to acknowledge that, by incorporating their business, the [owners] themselves created a distinct legal entity that has legally distinct rights and responsibilities from [its owners].[102]

The court emphasized that any penalties imposed by the contraceptive coverage mandate were the responsibility of the company, not its owners. Recognizing that, as the sole shareholders of the corporation, the owners of closely held corporations are impacted by the corporation's financial dealings, the court nonetheless found the distinction between the corporation and owners as separate legal parties significant.[103] Both the Third and Sixth Circuits emphasized that the benefits of incorporation include trade-offs for owners: "The corporate form offers several advantages 'not the least of which was limitation of liability,' but in return, the shareholder must give up some prerogatives, 'including that of direct legal action to redress an injury to him as primary stockholder in the business.'"[104]

## Rights of Corporate Owners with Religious Objections to Legislative Mandates

Because the Third and Sixth Circuits held that the corporations and their owners were separate legal entities, which were subject to distinct sets of legal rights, both courts rejected the owners' ability to challenge the mandate on behalf of their companies.[105] Standing to assert legal claims requires that a party be injured by the challenged action.[106] If the company is injured, it must seek redress for that injury itself, not through a third party, which is how those courts would characterize the owners of the company. As the Sixth Circuit explained, owners' actions "are not actions taken in an individual capacity, but as officers and directors of the corporation."[107] As such, they cannot be separated from the corporation for a distinct legal claim.

Other courts recognized the rights of the owners to assert a distinct claim related to their operation of their corporations. The D.C. Circuit held that secular organizations could not exercise religion and therefore could not pursue legal claims to protect any such right.[108] To determine whether the owners could assert a free exercise claim in their individual capacity, the court instead looked to the rules of shareholder standing, which generally prohibits shareholders from raising claims for injuries to the corporation.[109] The court held that the owners qualified for an exception to the rule because they were "injured in a way that is separate and distinct from an injury to the corporation," a conclusion with which the Seventh Circuit agreed.[110] The D.C. Circuit explained that "[i]f the companies have no claim to enforce—and as nonreligious corporations, they cannot engage in religious exercise—we are left with the obvious conclusion: the right belongs to the [owners], existing independently of any right of the ... companies."[111]

Noting the objections raised in other cases regarding the inherent trade-offs of incorporation, the D.C. Circuit reasoned that shareholders generally forgo certain rights in exchange for the benefits of incorporation because the company has the authority to exercise those rights on the shareholders behalf.[112] If the corporation cannot exercise a particular right, it would be unjust, according to the court, to refuse the owner's analogous right. Otherwise, "the price of incorporation [would be] not only the loss of RFRA's statutory free-exercise right, but the constitutional one as well. And that would create a risk of an unconstitutional condition in future cases."[113] The court therefore refused to hold that a person's statutory rights under RFRA depended on the form by which an individual chooses to operate his business.[114]

## Applying RFRA to Religious Objections to the Contraceptive Coverage Requirement

Of the five circuit courts that have considered contraceptive coverage cases, the Third and Sixth Circuits rejected the ability of the parties—either as corporations or their owners in their individual capacity—to challenge free exercise rights, and therefore did not address the likelihood on the parties' success on the merits. The remaining three circuits that found at least one party had standing to pursue the claim held that the claim was likely to succeed on the merits and granted a preliminary injunction preventing enforcement of the mandate with respect to those companies and individuals. Those courts considered the three elements of RFRA claims: whether the mandate imposed a substantial burden on religious exercise of the claimants; whether the government demonstrated a compelling interest in such a burden; and whether the government used the least restrictive means.

**Substantial Burden**

Courts generally have recognized the burden imposed by the contraceptive mandate on the companies as substantial, explaining that the significance of the penalties assessed for noncompliance with the contraceptive mandate—$100 per employee, per day of noncompliance—constituted substantial pressure on the company.[115] However, in its defense of the mandate, the government has alleged that the coverage requirements should not be considered to burden objecting employers' religious exercise. According to the government's arguments, the contraceptive requirement is not a direct burden. That is, it does not require any employer or employee who has an objection to the use of contraceptives to use or to encourage the use of such devices. The government instead has argued that the required insurance coverage is analogous to compensation, an issue on which the various challenging corporations do not have religious objections.[116] However, the courts have emphasized the deference due to religious objectors regarding the nature of their beliefs and related objections, citing the Supreme Court's long history of recognizing that it is not the role of the courts to determine the reasonableness of religious beliefs.[117]

In response to arguments that the mandate does not burden employers "because an employee's decision to use her insurance coverage to purchase contraception or sterilization services 'cannot be attributed to' the [owners of the corporations]," the Seventh Circuit elaborated on the deference owed to the corporations.[118] Echoing the D.C. Circuit's finding that the burden occurs when the employer must choose between managing a health plan that includes contraceptive coverage and paying penalties for a non-compliant plan, the court reasoned that the burden analysis should focus on the objection that the employer has to paying for coverage, not the employees' potential use of that coverage.[119] It emphasized that courts should not consider whether the employers' characterization of the religious conflict fits with the tenets of a particular religion or whether it is a reasonable or accurate religious belief.[120] The courts' assessment is consistent with Supreme Court jurisprudence and means that if an employer can demonstrate that its characterization of its objection is sincerely held, the requisite deference increases the probability that courts will find the employers' religious exercise is substantially burdened.[121]

**Compelling Interest**

Each of the courts considering the merits of the RFRA claims also found that the government's interest was not sufficiently compelling. The courts uniformly agreed that the government's justifications for the contraceptive coverage requirement—public health and gender equality— were too vague. The Tenth Circuit explained that the stated interests were too broadly formulated with no justification offered for the absence of specific exemptions in violation of the Supreme Court's decision in *Gonzales v. O Centro Espirita Beneficente Uniao do Vegetal.*[122] In that case, the Court explained that the government must provide a compelling interest if it offers an exception to one group but refuses to provide an exemption to another group from the same requirement.[123] The Tenth Circuit also explained that the interests could not be considered compelling because the requirement excluded tens of millions of people.[124]

The D.C. Circuit criticized the government's stated interests as "sketchy and highly abstract," explaining that there was an insufficient "nexus between this array of issues and the mandate."[125] For example, it suggested that public health may justify a number of governmental actions but the specific application of the contraceptive mandate did not achieve the goal of public health broadly.[126] However, the court did not foreclose the possibility that the government could show a compelling interest in maternal or fetal health.[127] The Seventh Circuit echoed the D.C. Circuit's criticism:

> By stating the public interests so generally, the government guarantees that the mandate will flunk the test. ... Stating the governmental interests at such a high level of generality makes it impossible to show that the mandate is the least restrictive means of furthering them. There are many ways to promote public health and gender equality, almost all of them less burdensome on religious liberty.[128]

**Least Restrictive Means**

The courts also rejected assertions that the mandate constituted the least restrictive means. The Seventh and D.C. Circuits noted that the government granted so many exceptions to the mandate that its arguments against exempting the companies with religious objections were unsustainable.[129] The D.C. Circuit noted that "[t]he regulatory scheme grandfathers, exempts, or 'accommodates' several categories of employers ... and does not apply to others (those with fewer than 50 employees."[130] It also noted that the government could use other methods to provide access to free contraceptive services without burdening the objectors, such as a public insurance option for contraceptive insurance; tax incentives to contraceptive providers who provide free services; and tax subsidies to individuals using contraceptive services, each of which would achieve the government's goal of facilitating access to contraceptive services while avoiding burdens posed on employers with objections.[131] The Tenth Circuit reasoned that litigants in that case requested exemption only from coverage of four of the twenty contraceptive methods required by the mandate and noted that the government failed to explain how the mandate "would be undermined" by granting such a limited exception.[132]

The D.C. Circuit reasoned that the government had failed to justify its refusal to offer an exemption, noting that an exemption claimed on similar grounds was claimed in *United States v. Lee*. *Lee* involved a challenge to the social security tax program and the Supreme Court held that providing the exemption requested would make the program unworkable and therefore undermine the government's interest in effectively administering the program. In the contraceptive mandate case, the D.C. Circuit explained that "there is nothing to suggest that the preventive-care statute would become unworkable if employers objecting on religious grounds could opt out of one part of a comprehensive coverage requirement," noting that the company's employees would still be eligible for a wide range of preventive health services also required by the statute.[133]

## Supreme Court Review of *Conestoga* and *Hobby Lobby Stores*

On November 26, 2013, the Supreme Court agreed to review *Conestoga* and *Hobby Lobby Stores*. The two cases have been consolidated, with one hour of oral argument scheduled for both cases. The Court appears poised to address both the constitutional and statutory questions raised by ACA's contraceptive coverage requirement. A decision that recognizes the free exercise rights of secular, for-profit corporations would likely have an impact beyond the ACA requirement, and could lead to such corporations seeking exemptions from other requirements.

The Court's interest in the free exercise issues raised by *Conestoga* and *Hobby Lobby Stores* was further demonstrated in *Little Sisters of the Poor Home for the Aged v. Sebelius.*[134] Unlike Conestoga Wood Specialties Corporation and Hobby Lobby Stores, Little Sisters of the Poor Home for the Aged is a nonprofit entity that could arguably seek an accommodation in connection with the contraceptive coverage requirement. The organization argued, however, that signing and providing the self-certification form that is needed for an accommodation would violate its religious beliefs.[135] In January 2014, the Court enjoined the Department of Health and Human Services (HHS) from enforcing the contraceptive coverage requirement against Little Sisters of the Poor Home for the Aged pending final disposition by the Tenth Circuit if it informed the HHS Secretary in writing that it was a nonprofit organization with religious objections to providing contraceptive services. The Court indicated that the organization did not have to use the self-certification form prescribed by the federal government.[136]

## End Notes

[1] Patient Protection and Affordable Care Act, P.L. 111-148, §1001(5), 111th Cong., 2nd Sess. (2010). ACA was amended by the Health Care Education and Reconciliation Act of 2010 (HCERA; P.L. 111-152) (2010). These acts will be collectively referred to in this report as "ACA."

[2] *See* Hobby Lobby Stores v. Sebelius, 723 F.3d 1114 (10th Cir. 2013), *cert. granted*, 2013 U.S. LEXIS 8418 (November 26, 2013) (No. 13-354); Conestoga Wood Specialties Corp. v. Secretary of U.S. Department of Health and Human Services, 724 F.3d 377 (3rd Cir. 2013), *cert. granted*, 2013 U.S. LEXIS 8419 (November 26, 2013) (No. 13- 354); Autocam Corp. v. Sebelius, No. 12-2673, 2013 U.S. App. LEXIS 19152 (6th Cir. 2013); Gilardi v. U.S. Department of Health and Human Services, No. 13-5069, 2013 U.S. App. LEXIS 22256 (D.C. Cir. 2013); Korte v. Sebelius, Nos. 12-3841 & 13-1077, 2013 U.S. App. LEXIS 22748 (7th Cir. 2013).

[3] *See, e.g.*, 42 U.S.C. §2000e-1(a) (exempting any "religious corporation, association, educational institution, or society" from prohibition on employment discrimination based on religion); 26 U.S.C. §1402(g) (exempting individuals who are members of religious sects having beliefs in conflict with the acceptance of insurance benefits from self-employment tax requirements).

[4] *See* Bernstein v. Ocean Grove Camp Meeting Association, No. PN34XB-03008 (N.J. Office of Administrative Law, January 12, 2012); Elane Photography v. Willock, No. 33,687, 2013 N.M. LEXIS 284 (N.M. 2013).

[5] *Supra* notes 2 and 4.

[6] Reynolds v. United States, 98 U.S. 145, 162-64 (1879).

[7] *Id.* at 166 ("Laws are made for the government of actions, and while they cannot interfere with mere religious belief and opinions, they may with practices."). *See also* Cantwell v.

Connecticut, 310 U.S. 296, 303 (1940) ("[T]he [First] Amendment embraces two concepts,—freedom to belief and freedom to act.").

[8] *See, e.g.*, Religious Freedom Restoration Act of 1993, P.L. 103-141, 103rd Cong., 1st Sess. (November 16, 1993), codified at 42 U.S.C. §§2000bb et seq.

[9] U.S. Const., amend. I.

[10] *See* Sherbert v. Verner, 374 U.S. 398 (1963); Wisconsin v. Yoder, 406 U.S. 205 (1972).

[11] 494 U.S. 872, 879 (1990) (internal quotes omitted).

[12] *Id.* at 890.

[13] P.L. 103-141, 103rd Cong., 1st Sess. (1993), codified at 42 U.S.C. §2000bb et seq.

[14] 42 U.S.C. §2000bb-1(b).

[15] *See* City of Boerne v. Flores, 521 U.S. 507 (1997).

[16] Generally, under the legal principle of entrenchment, a legislative action cannot bind a future Congress. That is, Congress cannot entrench a legislative action by providing that it may not be repealed or altered. *See* Fletcher v. Peck, 10 U.S. 87, 135 (Chief Justice Marshall) ("The principle asserted is, that one legislature is competent to repeal any act which a former legislature was competent to pass; and that one legislature cannot abridge the powers of a succeeding legislature."). The U.S. Supreme Court has noted the long history of this rule. *See* United States v. Winstar Corp., 518 U.S. 839, 872-74 (1996).

[17] *See, e.g.*, Watson v. Jones, 80 U.S. 679, 728-29 (1872).

[18] *See* Lemon v. Kurtzman, 403 U.S. 602 (1971). The tripartite *Lemon* test has traditionally been used by the Court to determine whether a governmental action comports with the Establishment Clause. It requires that a challenged law (1) have a secular purpose; (2) have a neutral primary effect; and (3) not foster excessive entanglement with religion. *Id.* at 612-13.

[19] United States v. Ballard, 322 U.S. 78, 86-87 (1944).

[20] *See* United States v. Seeger, 380 U.S. 163, 185 (1965); Welsh v. United States 398 U.S. 333, 339-40 (1970). *See also* Quaring v. Peterson, 728 F.2d 1121 (8th Cir. 1984).

[21] P.L. 88-352, Title VII, 78 Stat. 253, codified at 42 U.S.C. §§2000e et seq.

[22] 42 U.S.C. §2000e(j).

[23] 29 C.F.R. §1605.1. *See also Seeger*, 380 U.S. 163; *Welsh*, 398 U.S. 333.

[24] *See* Epperson v. Arkansas, 393 U.S. 97, 104 (1968). *See also* Wallace v. Jaffree, 472 U.S. 38, 52-54 (1985); School Dist. of Abington Township v. Schempp, 374 U.S. 203, 216-217 (1963); Church of the Lukumi Babalu Aye v. City of Hialeah, 508 U.S. 520 (1993).

[25] 42 U.S.C. §2000e-2.

[26] *Id. See also* 42 U.S.C. §2000e(j).

[27] 42 U.S.C. §2000e-1(a).

[28] 42 U.S.C. §2000e-2(e)(2).

[29] Spencer v. World Vision, Inc., 633 F.3d 723, 724 (9th Cir. 2011) (per curiam), *cert. denied*, 132 S.Ct. 96 (2011).

[30] *See, e.g.*, LeBoon v. Lancaster Jewish Community Center Association, 503 F.3d 217, 226-27 (3rd Cir. 2007) (providing a summary discussion of the circuit courts' interpretations of which organizations qualify for exemption under Title VII).

[31] *See* 42 U.S.C. §300gg-13.

[32] *See* 75 Fed. Reg. 41,733. See also Jacobson v. Massachusetts, 197 U.S. 11 (1905); Catholic Charities of Sacramento v. Superior Court, 85 P.3d 67 (Cal. 2004); Catholic Charities of the Diocese of Albany v. Serio, 859 N.E.2d 459 (N.Y. 2006).

[33] Coverage of Certain Preventive Health Services Under the Affordable Care Act, 78 Fed. Reg. 39,870 (July 2, 2013).

[34] 45 C.F.R. §147.131(a).

[35] *Id.*

[36] 26 U.S.C. §6033(a)(3)(A)(i), (iii).

[37] 45 C.F.R. §147.131(c)(2).

[38] 45 C.F.R. §147.131(b).

[39] Dozens of lawsuits have been filed challenging the contraceptive coverage requirement under the First Amendment and RFRA with mixed success. Cases may be tracked at HHS Mandate Information Central, The Becket Fund for Religious Liberty, *available at* http://www.becketfund.org/hhsinformationcentral/.

[40] P.L. 88-352, Title II, 88th Cong., 2nd Sess. (1964), codified at 42 U.S.C. §§2000a et seq.

[41] 42 U.S.C. §2000a(b).

[42] *See* 42 U.S.C. §2000a(a).

[43] The scope of state protections against discrimination by public accommodations based on sexual orientation varies. For a review of states that have included sexual orientation as a protected class under public accommodations laws, see LGBT-Inclusive Public Accommodations Laws, Human Rights Campaign, *available at* http://www.hrc.org /resources/ entry/lgbt-inclusive-public-accommodations-laws1.

[44] *See, e.g.,* Bernstein v. Ocean Grove Camp Meeting Association, No. PN34XB-03008 (N.J. Office of Administrative Law, January 12, 2012); Elane Photography v. Willock, No. 33,687, 2013 N.M. LEXIS 284 (N.M. 2013).

[45] *See* Jerry Filteau, *Catholic Charities in Boston Archdiocese to End Adoption Services*, Catholic News Service (March 13, 2006), *available at* http://www.catholicnews.com/data /stories/cns/0601456.htm; North Coast Women's Care Medical Group, Inc. v. Superior Court of San Diego County, 189 P.3d 959 (Cal. 2008) (holding Free Exercise rights do not exempt physicians from complying with state nondiscrimination laws prohibiting discrimination based on sexual orientation); Levin v. Yeshiva University, 754 N.E.2d 1099 (N.Y. 2001) (challenging university's decision to deny housing to homosexual couple).

[46] *See, e.g.,* N.H. Rev. Stat. Ann. §457:37; Conn. Gen. Stat. §46b-35a.

[47] *See, e.g.,* Bernstein v. Ocean Grove Camp Meeting Association, No. PN34XB-03008 (N.J. Office of Administrative Law, January 12, 2012).

[48] *See, e.g., Sherbert*, 374 U.S. 398; Corp. of the Presiding Bishop of the Church of Jesus Christ of Latter-Day Saints v. Amos, 483 U.S. 327 (1987).

[49] *See* Hobby Lobby Stores v. Sebelius, 723 F.3d 1114 (10th Cir. 2013), *cert. granted,* 2013 U.S. LEXIS 8418 (November 26, 2013) (No. 13-354); Conestoga Wood Specialties Corp. v. Secretary of U.S. Department of Health and Human Services, 724 F.3d 377 (3rd Cir. 2013), *cert. granted,* 2013 U.S. LEXIS 8419 (November 26, 2013) (No. 13- 354); Autocam Corp. v. Sebelius, No. 12-2673, 2013 U.S. App. LEXIS 19152 (6th Cir. 2013); Gilardi v. U.S. Department of Health and Human Services, No. 13-5069, 2013 U.S. App. LEXIS 22256 (D.C. Cir. 2013); Korte v. Sebelius, Nos. 12-3841 & 13-1077, 2013 U.S. App. LEXIS 22748 (7th Cir. 2013).

[50] *Korte*, 2013 U.S. App. LEXIS 22748; *Hobby Lobby Stores*, 723 F.3d 1114; *Gilardi*, 2013 U.S. App. LEXIS 22256.

[51] *Conestoga*, 724 F.3d 377; *Autocam Corp.*, 2013 U.S. App. LEXIS 19152.

[52] Only one company provides products explicitly related to religion, but it is not considered a religious organization. *See Hobby Lobby Stores*, 723 F.3d 1114 (challenge by owners of two companies, including a craft store chain and a Christian bookstore chain).

[53] Equal Employment Opportunity Commission v. Townley Engineering & Manufacturing Co., 859 F.2d 610 (9th Cir. 1988).

[54] *Id.* at 618.
[55] *Id.* at 619.
[56] *Id.*
[57] *Id.*
[58] *Id.* at 620.
[59] *Id.* at 621.
[60] *Id.*
[61] *Id.*
[62] *Smith*, 494 U.S. at 890.
[63] 42 U.S.C. §2000bb-1(a).
[64] 1 U.S.C. §1.
[65] *Conestoga*, 724 F.3d 377; *Autocam Corp.*, 2013 U.S. App. LEXIS 19152.
[66] *Autocam Corp.*, 2013 U.S. App. LEXIS 19152 at 21-22.
[67] *Autocam Corp.*, 2013 U.S. App. LEXIS 19152 at 22.
[68] *Autocam Corp.*, 2013 U.S. App. LEXIS 19152 at 22-23.
[69] *Hobby Lobby Stores*, 723 F.3d 1114.
[70] *Hobby Lobby Stores*, 723 F.3d at 1129; *Korte*, 2013 U.S. App. LEXIS 22748 at 49-52.
[71] *Id.*
[72] *Korte*, 2013 U.S. App. LEXIS 22748 at 53.
[73] *Id.* at 54-55.
[74] *See Hobby Lobby Stores*, 723 F.3d at 1136-37.
[75] *Id.*
[76] *Conestoga*, 724 F.3d 377; *Autocam Corp.*, 2013 U.S. App. LEXIS 19152.
[77] *Korte*, 2013 U.S. App. LEXIS 22748 at 64-65.
[78] *Id.* at 65.
[79] *Id.* at 65-66 (citing Thomas v. Review Board of the Indiana Employment Security Division, 450 U.S. 707 (1981) and *Sherbert*, 374 U.S. 398).
[80] *Korte*, 2013 U.S. App. LEXIS 22748 at 66-67 (citing Braunfeld v. Brown, 366 U.S. 599 (1961)).
[81] *See* 455 U.S. 252 (1982).
[82] *Korte*, 2013 U.S. App. LEXIS 22748 at 68.
[83] *Hobby Lobby Stores*, 723 F.3d at 1134-35.
[84] *Conestoga*, 724 F.3d 377; *Autocam Corp.*, 2013 U.S. App. LEXIS 19152; *Gilardi*, 2013 U.S. App. LEXIS 22256.
[85] *Hobby Lobby Stores*, 723 F.3d 1114; *Korte*, 2013 U.S. App. LEXIS 22748.
[86] 558 U.S. 310, 342 (2010).
[87] *Id.* at 343.
[88] *Hobby Lobby Stores*, 723 F.3d at 1134 (internal quotations and citations omitted).
[89] *Id.* at 1134-35.
[90] *Hobby Lobby Stores*, 723 F.3d at 1135 (internal citation omitted).
[91] *Korte*, 2013 U.S. App. LEXIS 22748 at 71-73.
[92] *Conestoga*, 724 F.3d at 386.
[93] *Id.* at 384.
[94] *Gilardi*, 2013 U.S. App. LEXIS 22256 at 9 (noting that RFRA does not clarify the meaning of person or exercise of religion, and explaining that it must examine "the full body of our free-exercise caselaw to discern whether the [companies qualify for protection] under the statute").
[95] *Id.* at 13.

[96] *Id.* at 16.
[97] *Townley*, 859 F.2d at 619-20.
[98] Stormans v. Selecky, 586 F.3d 1109, 1119 (9th Cir. 2009).
[99] *Id.* at 1120.
[100] *Gilardi*, 2013 U.S. App. LEXIS 22256 at 18.
[101] *Id.* at 18-20.
[102] *Conestoga*, 724 F.3d at 387-88 (internal citations omitted).
[103] *Id.* at 388.
[104] *Id. See also Autocam Corp.*, 2013 U.S. App. LEXIS 19152 at 15.
[105] *Conestoga*, 724 F.3d 377; *Autocam Corp.*, 2013 U.S. App. LEXIS 19152.
[106] There are generally three constitutionally required elements to standing: (1) the individual must have personally suffered an actual or threatened injury; (2) the injury must be fairly traced to the challenged action; and (3) the injury must be likely to be redressed by a favorable decision. *See* Valley Forge Christian College v. Americans United for Separation of Church and State, 454 U.S. 464, 472 (1982); Allen v. Wright, 468 U.S. 737, 751 (1984); Lujan v. Defenders of Wildlife, 504 U.S. 555, 560-61 (1992).
[107] *Autocam Corp.*, 2013 U.S. App. LEXIS 19152 at 14.
[108] *Gilardi*, 2013 U.S. App. LEXIS 22256 at 20.
[109] *Id.* at 20-22.
[110] *Id.* at 21 (quotation and citation omitted). *See also Korte*, 2013 U.S. App. LEXIS 22748 at 32-34.
[111] *Gilardi*, 2013 U.S. App. LEXIS 22256 at 22.
[112] *Id.* at 27-28.
[113] *Id.* at 30.
[114] *Id.* at 29.
[115] *Hobby Lobby Stores*, 723 F.3d at 1140. *See also Korte*, 2013 U.S. App. LEXIS 22748 at 76-77.
[116] *Hobby Lobby Stores*, 723 F.3d at 1141.
[117] *Id.* at 1141.
[118] *Korte*, 2013 U.S. App. LEXIS 22748 at 78.
[119] *Id.* at 80-81. *See also Gilardi*, 2013 U.S. App. LEXIS 22256 at 24-25.
[120] *Korte*, 2013 U.S. App. LEXIS 22748 at 81-82.
[121] As discussed earlier in this report, courts assess the sincerity of religious beliefs by determining whether the objector adheres to the belief consistently in his or her practices. In other words, it cannot be an objection established with the ulterior motive of avoiding compliance with an unpopular mandate.
[122] *Hobby Lobby Stores*, 723 F.3d at 1143-44.
[123] 546 U.S. 418 (2006).
[124] *Hobby Lobby Stores*, 723 F.3d at 1143.
[125] *Gilardi*, 2013 U.S. App. LEXIS 22256 at 33.
[126] *Id.* at 33-34.
[127] *Id.* at 38.
[128] *Korte*, 2013 U.S. App. LEXIS 22748 at 84.
[129] *Id.* at 85; *Gilardi*, 2013 U.S. App. LEXIS 22256 at 41 (noting that because of the large numbers already exempt from regulation, "the mandate is unquestionably underinclusive").
[130] *Korte*, 2013 U.S. App. LEXIS 22748 at 85-86.
[131] *Id.* at 86.
[132] Hobby Lobby Stores, 723 F.3d at 1144.

[133] *Gilardi*, 2013 U.S. App. LEXIS 22256 at 44-45.

[134] 134 S.Ct. 1022 (2014).

[135] *See* Emergency Appl. for Inj. Pending Appellate Review or, in the Alternative, Pet. for Writ of Cert. and Inj. Pending Resolution, Little Sisters of the Poor Home for the Aged v. Sebelius, Nos. 13A691 (S.Ct. December 31, 2013), *available at* http://www.becketfund.org/wp-content/uploads/2013/12/Little-Sisters-v-Sebelius-Supreme-CourtInjunction-Application.pdf.

[136] *See* note 134.

# INDEX

## A



## B



## C

## D



## E



## F

## G



## H



## I

## J



## K



## L



## M



## N

## O



## P



## Q



## R

## V



## W